D0621920

In the middle of the bowl is what looks like a gigantic statue of a snake's head, its mouth open, showing great curving fangs. Tyutchev does not hesitate, for there is no other way out of the cavern. He leaps into the statue's open mouth and is lost to view. You sprint towards the statue as the Krathak's stinking breath bathes you and its footfalls shake the earth…

Gamebooks from Fabled Lands Publishing

by Jamie Thomson and Dave Morris:

Fabled Lands 1: The War-Torn Kingdom
Fabled Lands 2: Cities of Gold and Glory
Fabled Lands 3: Over the Blood-Dark Sea
Fabled Lands 4: The Plains of Howling Darkness
Fabled Lands 5: The Court of Hidden Faces
Fabled Lands 6: Lords of the Rising Sun

by Dave Morris:

Heart of Ice
Down Among the Dead Men
Necklace of Skulls
Once Upon a Time in Arabia
Crypt of the Vampire
The Temple of Flame
The Castle of Lost Souls

by Oliver Johnson:

Curse of the Pharaoh
The Lord of Shadow Keep

by Dave Morris and Oliver Johnson:

Blood Sword 1: The Battlepits of Krarth
Blood Sword 2: The Kingdom of Wyrd
Blood Sword 3: The Demon's Claw
Blood Sword 4: Doomwalk

by Jamie Thomson and Mark Smith:

Way of the Tiger 1: Avenger
Way of the Tiger 2: Assassin
Way of the Tiger 3: Usurper
Way of the Tiger 4: Overlord
Way of the Tiger 5: Warbringer
Way of the Tiger 6: Inferno

Way of the Tiger
INFERNO!

JAMIE THOMSON
& MARK SMITH

FL

Originally published 1987 by Knight Books
This edition published 2014 by Fabled Lands Publishing
an imprint of Fabled Lands LLP

www.sparkfurnace.com

Text copyright © 1987, 2014 Mark Smith and Jamie Thomson

Interior illustrations by Sebastien Brunet and Hokusai

Cover by Mylène Villeneuve

Irsmuncast map by Leo Hartas

Edited by Richard S. Hetley

With thanks to Mikaël Louys, Michael Spencelayh, Paul Gresty
and David Walters

The rights of Jamie Thomson and Mark Smith to be identified as
the authors of this work have been asserted by them in
accordance with the Copyright, Designs and Patents Act 1988.

ISBN-13: 978-1-909905-15-3
ISBN-10: 1909905151

WARNING!

Do not attempt any of the techniques or methods described in this book. They could result in serious injury or death to an untrained user.

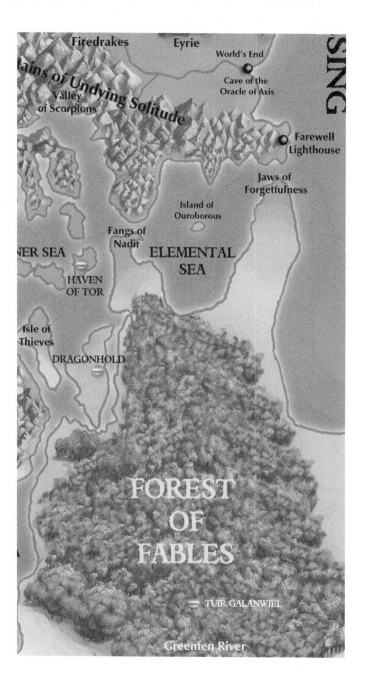

Firedrakes

Eyrie

World's End

Cave of the
Oracle of Axis

...tains of Undying Solitude

Valley
of Scorpions

Farewell
Lighthouse

Jaws of
Forgetfulness

Island of
Ouroborous

Fangs of
Nadir

ELEMENTAL
SEA

...NER SEA

HAVEN
OF TOR

Isle of
Thieves

DRAGONHOLD

FOREST

OF

FABLES

TUIR GALANWIEL

Greenfen River

Ninja Character Sheet

Combat Ratings							
Punch	0						
Kick	0						
Throw	0						
Fate Modifier	0						

Skills   + Shurikenjutsu

Endurance

STARTS AT 20

Inner Force

STARTS AT 5

NINJA TOOLS

NINJA COSTUME

BREATHING TUBE

IRON SLEEVES

GAROTTE

FLASH POWDER

FLINT & TINDER

SPIDERFISH

BLOOD OF NIL

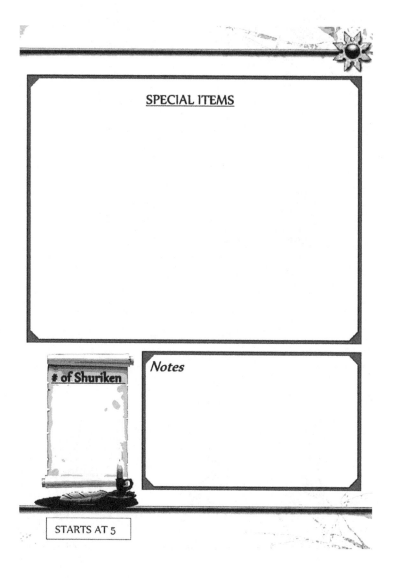

SPECIAL ITEMS

of Shuriken

Notes

STARTS AT 5

Winged Horse Kick

Leaping Tiger Kick

1

2

Forked Lightning Kick

Iron Fist Punch

Tiger's Paw Punch

Cobra Strike
Punch

Whirlpool Throw

Dragon's Tail Throw

Teeth of Tiger Throw

Opponent Encounter Boxes

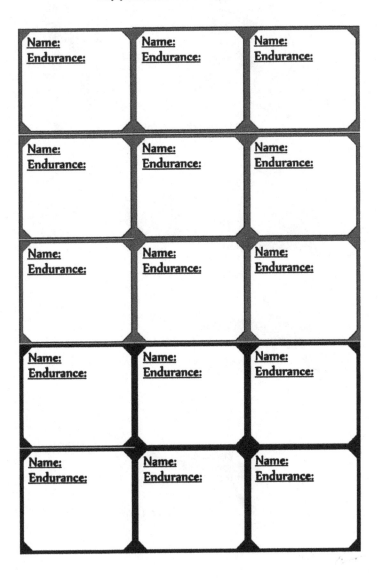

Name:
Endurance:

Name:
Endurance:

Name:
Endurance:

Name:
Endurance:

Name:
Endurance:

Name:
Endurance:

Name:
Endurance:

Name:
Endurance:

Name:
Endurance:

Name:
Endurance:

Name:
Endurance:

Name:
Endurance:

Name:
Endurance:

Name:
Endurance:

Name:
Endurance:

BACKGROUND

On the magical world of Orb, alone in a sea that the people of the Manmarch call Endless, lies the mystical Island of Tranquil Dreams.

Many years have passed since the time when you first saw its golden shores and emerald rice meadows. A servant brought you, braving the distant leagues of the ponderous ocean from lands to which you have never returned. Your loyal servant laid you, an orphan, at the steps of the Temple of the Rock praying that the monks would care for you, for she was frail and dying of a hideous curse.

Monks have lived on the island for centuries, dedicated to the worship of their God, Kwon, He who speaks the Holy Words of Power, Supreme Master of Unarmed Combat. They live only to help others resist the evil that infests the world. Seeing that you were alone and needed care, the monks took you in and you became an acolyte at the Temple of the Rock. Nothing was made of the strange birthmark, shaped like a crown, which you carry on your thigh, though you remember that the old servant insisted that it was of mystical importance. Whenever you have asked about this the monks have bade you meditate and be patient.

The most ancient and powerful of them all, Naijishi, Grandmaster of the Dawn, became your foster-father. He gave you guidance and training in the calm goodness of Kwon, knowledge of men and their ways and how to meditate so that your mind floats free of your body and rides the winds in search of truth.

From the age of six, however, most of your time has been spent learning the Way of the Tiger. Now you are a ninja, a master of the martial arts and a deadly assassin who can kill the most powerful enemies unseen and unsuspected. Like a tiger, you are strong, stealthy, agile, patient in the stalking of prey and deadly. On the Island of Plenty and in the Manmarch the fabled ninja, known as the 'Men with no Shadow', are held in awe – the mere mention of ninja strikes fear into people's hearts. But you are one of the few who worship Kwon and follow the Way of the Tiger. You use your skill as a bringer of death to rid the world of evil-doers.

At an early age you hung by the hands for hours on end from the branches of trees to strengthen your arms. You ran for miles, your light-footed speed enough to keep a thirty-foot ribbon trailing above the ground. You trod tightropes, as agile as a monkey. Now you swim like a fish and leap like a tiger, you move like the whisper of the breeze and glide through the blackest night like a shade. Before he died, Naijishi taught you the Ninja's Covenant.

NINJA NO CHIGIRI

'I will vanish into the night; change my body to wood or stone; sink into the earth and walk through walls and locked doors. I will be killed many times, yet will not die; change my face and become invisible, able to walk among men without being seen.'

It was after your foster-father Naijishi's death that you began to live the words of the Covenant. A man came to the island, Yaemon, Grandmaster of Flame. Using borrowed sorcery he tricked the monks into believing that he was a worshipper of Kwon from the Greater Continent. He was indeed a monk but he worshipped Kwon's twisted brother, Vile, who helps the powerful to subdue the weak, and wicked men to rule fools. Yaemon slew Naijishi – no one could match him in unarmed combat – and he stole the Scrolls of Kettsuin from the Temple. Once more you knew the pain of loss for you had loved Naijishi as a father. You swore an oath to Kwon that one day you would avenge his death . . . and you *were* avenged. You slew Yaemon and you learned of your ancestry, of the significance of the birthmark carried by the first-born of your family for four generations. Now you are King of the City of Irsmuncast.

KING OF IRSMUNCAST

You gathered advisors around you and passed many new laws, some popular, others less than popular, but you managed to govern the city, playing one faction off against another until Irsmuncast came under attack. Not for nothing is the city named Irsmuncast nigh Edge. Its location at the eastern edge of the Manmarch, the lands of men, means that whenever the hosts of evil spew forth from the Bowels of Orb, the great Rift that scores the world like a black pit in a rotten fruit, it is likely that Irsmuncast will be the city they fall upon in their search for new slaves. And so it was early in your reign. The army repulsed them once, but, prompted by your god Kwon the Redeemer, you set out on a quest to recover the Orb and Sceptre which are the traditional emblems of your family's rule. The quest was successful, though it cost you your left eye. Touching the Sceptre transported you magically back to the battlemented tower of the Palace where a terrible sight met your weakened gaze. The city was wreathed in smoke, torched by the evil hordes from the Rift.

You repelled the first invasion and restored your sight by replacing your lost eye with the Orb. With both magic and might of arms, you then led your forces in a great struggle against the forces of evil and triumphed in the final battle. Your arch enemy Honoric and the dread Legion of the Sword of Doom were crushed and the Spawn of the Rift crept back to their underground fastnesses far from the sunlit lands of men, but they have not forgotten you.

PEACE IN THE MANMARCH

On your triumphal return to the city, the streets of Irsmuncast had been strewn with flowers. Your victory against Honoric and the Legion of the Sword of Doom has made you the darling of the people. The months that follow are among the happiest of your life. As Overlord you will never be carefree, but your reign is now blessed with peace both within and without the city walls. The forces of the Rift had largely melted away when news of Honoric's defeat reached them and there have been no more raids from the Rift, the gaping chasm that men call the Bowels of Orb, since that glorious day. Your friends Glaivas the Ranger-Lord and the Paladin, Doré le Jeune, became themselves fast friends during the celebrations, and at the zealous Paladin's suggestion, and against his better judgement, Glaivas allowed himself to be persuaded to accompany Doré on a punitive expedition to the Rift. They left almost a month ago to the day, and are due to arrive back at court after the first day of Pantheos.

Gwyneth, Force-Lady of the shieldmaidens of Dama, continues to oversee the keeping of law and of the military with her customary efficiency, and the Demagogue has persuaded you to sponsor a series of new buildings which he hopes will spark a renaissance for the city. The treasury is empty and you have had to borrow to make payments to the dependants of those killed in the war, but the people are happy. Your allies have returned home with gifts to show that they can count on you for allegiance should they ever fall under attack.

The Manmarch is at peace. Still, you begin to feel increasingly uneasy as the month of Pantheos arrives and the days continue to pass.

RULES OF COMBAT

As a master of Taijutsu, the ninja's art of unarmed combat, you have four main ways of fighting: throwing shuriken (see under skills), kicks, punches and throws.

In general it is harder to hit an opponent when kicking but a kick does more damage than a punch. A throw, if successful, allows you to follow up with a possible 'killing blow', but if you fail an attempt to throw an opponent, your Defence against the opponent will be lower, as you are open to attack. Shuriken are a special case and will be mentioned in the text when you can use them.

Whenever you are in a combat you will be asked which type of attack you wish to make. See the Way of the Tiger illustrations for the different types of kicks, punches and throws available to you. Think about your opponent and its likely fighting style. Trying to throw a giant enemy is not going to be as easy as throwing an ordinary man, for example. You will be told which paragraph to turn to, depending on your choice.

When you are resolving combat, you will find it useful to record your opponent's current Endurance score. A number of Encounter Boxes are provided with your Character Sheet for this purpose.

The combats have been presented in such a way that it is possible for you to briefly examine the rules and begin play almost immediately, but fighting is tactical. Do not forget the rules for blocking and Inner Force (see below), as you will rarely be told when to use these in the text.

PUNCH

When you try to strike an enemy with a punch, that enemy will have a Defence number. You need to score higher than this number on the roll of two dice (an Attack Roll). You get to add your Punch Modifier (see below) to this roll. If the score is higher than his or her Defence number, you have punched your opponent successfully. In this case, roll one more die. The result is the amount of damage you have inflicted on your opponent. Every opponent has Endurance or 'hit points'. The damage you do is subtracted from your opponent's Endurance total. If this has reduced your opponent's score to 0 or less, you have won.

Punch Modifier: Whenever you make an Attack Roll to determine whether or not you have successfully punched an opponent, add or subtract your Punch Modifier. This number reflects your skill in using the punches of the Way of the Tiger. Your starting Punch Modifier is 0, as noted on your Character Sheet. This may change during the adventure.

The Enemy's Attack: After you punch, any opponent still in the fight will counter attack. You will be given your Defence number. Roll two dice, and if the score is greater than your Defence, you have been hit. The amount of damage inflicted upon you depends on the opponent and will be noted in the text, in a format such as 'Damage: 1 Die + 1' or '2 Dice' or '1 Die + 2'. Simply roll the required number of dice and add any other number given. This is the total damage inflicted upon you. However, before you subtract this score from your Endurance, you may choose to try and block or parry the attack (see block) to prevent any damage.

KICK
The kick and the Kick Modifier work exactly as the punch, except that a kick will do 2 more points of damage than a punch ('1 Die + 2'). It will often be harder to hit with a kick. If the opponent survives, he or she will counter attack.

THROW
The throw and Throw Modifier work as the punch to determine success. A throw does no damage to your foe; instead, you will be allowed another attack, a punch or kick, with a +2 bonus to hit (like an extra Punch Modifier or Kick Modifier) and +2 to damage. (All bonuses are cumulative – a kick normally does '1 Die + 2' damage, so after a successful throw it does '1 Die + 4'.) The opponent will only counter attack against a throw if you fail.

ENDURANCE

You begin the game with 20 points of Endurance. Keep a running total of your Endurance on your Character Sheet. It will probably be the number that will change most as you are wounded, healed etc. When you reach 0 Endurance or less, you are dead and your adventure ends. When restoring Endurance, you cannot go above your maximum of 20.

BLOCK

As a ninja, a master of Taijutsu, you have the ability to block or parry incoming blows with various parts of your body, often your forearms. For this purpose, thin lightweight iron rods have been sewn into your sleeves enabling you to block even swords and other weapons. During combat, if you have been hit, you may try to block the blow and take no damage. Roll two dice. If the score is less than your Defence given in that combat, you have successfully blocked the blow, and take no damage. If your score is equal to or greater than your Defence, you take damage in the normal way. In any case, because you have taken the time to block, your next attack will be less effective, as your opponent has had more time to react. Whether your block is successful or not, −2 will be applied to your Punch, Kick and Throw Modifier for your next attack only. Remember, you can only block blows, not missiles or magic.

INNER FORCE

You begin the adventure with 5 points of Inner Force. Through meditation and rigorous training you have mastered the ability to unleash spiritual or inner power through your body in the same way as the karate experts of today break blocks of wood and bricks. In any combat, before you roll the dice to determine if you will hit or miss an opponent, you may choose to use Inner Force. If you do, deduct one point from your Inner Force score. This is used up whether or not you succeed in striking your opponent. If you are successful, however, double the damage you inflict – first make your roll for damage and add any bonus (e.g., '1 Die + 2' for a kick), then double the result. When your Inner

Force is reduced to 0, you cannot use Inner Force again until you find some way to restore it – so use it wisely. When restoring Inner Force, you cannot go above your maximum of 5.

FATE

Luck plays its part and the goddess Fate has great power on the world of Orb. Whenever you are asked to make a Fate Roll, roll two dice, adding or subtracting your Fate Modifier. If the score is 7–12, you are lucky and Fate has smiled on you. If the score is 2–6, you are unlucky and Fate has turned her back on you. You begin your adventure with a Fate Modifier of 0. Later on, this might go up or down, as you are blessed or cursed by Fate.

NINJA TOOLS

As well as any equipment you may take depending on your skills (see next), as a ninja you have certain tools with you from the beginning. These are:

THE NINJA COSTUME

During the day you would normally be disguised as a traveller, beggar or suchlike. At night when on a mission, you would wear costume. This consists of a few pieces of black cloth. One piece is worn as a jacket covering the chest and arms, two others are wound around each leg and held in at the waist. Finally, a long piece of cloth is wrapped around the head, leaving only the eyes exposed. The reverse side of the costume can be white, for travel on snowy ground, or green, for travel in woods or grasslands.

IRON SLEEVES
Sewn into the sleeves of your costume are four thin strips of iron, the length of your forearm. These allow you to parry or block blows from swords and other cutting weapons.

BREATHING TUBE
Made from bamboo, this can be used as a snorkel allowing you to remain underwater for long periods of time. It can also be used as a blow-pipe in conjunction with the Poison Needles skill, for added range.

GARROTTE
A specialised killing tool of the ninja, this is a length of wire used to assassinate enemies by strangulation.

FLASH POWDER
This powder, when thrown in any source of flame, causes a blinding flash. You have enough for one use only.

FLINT AND TINDER
Used for making fires.

SPIDERFISH
Salted and cured, this highly venomous fish is used as a source for the deadly poison used in conjunction with the Poison Needles skill, and as a useful way of removing any guardian beasts or animals.

THE BLOOD OF NIL
You also carry one dose of the most virulent poison known on Orb. This venom is extremely difficult and very dangerous to collect for it is taken from the barb of a scorpion son of the God, Nil, Mouth of the Void. You had used yours long ago, but have found a replacement amongst the bizarre and otherworldly treasures hoarded by the evil Usurper.

THE SKILLS OF THE WAY OF THE TIGER

You have been trained in ninjutsu almost all of your life. Your senses of smell, sight and hearing have been honed to almost superhuman effectiveness. You are well versed in woodcraft, able to track like a bloodhound, and to cover your own tracks. Your knowledge of plants and herb lore enables you to live off the land. You are at the peak of physical fitness, able to run up to 50 miles a day and swim like a fish. Your training included horsemanship, a little ventriloquism, meditation, the ability to hold yourself absolutely still for hours on end, perfecting your balance, and 'The Seven Ways of Going' or disguise. The latter skill involves comprehensive training so that you can perform as a minstrel, for instance, if this disguise is used. However, a major part of this training has been stealth, hiding in shadows, moving silently, and breathing as quietly as possible, enabling you to move about unseen and unheard. You begin the game with these skills.

There are nine other skills. One of these, Shurikenjutsu, is always taught to a ninja in training. This you must take, but you may then choose three other skills from the remaining eight, and note them on your Character Sheet.

SHURIKENJUTSU

You begin the adventure with five shuriken. The type you specialise in are 'throwing stars', small razor-sharp star-shaped disks of metal. You can throw these up to a range of about thirty feet with devastating effect. If you throw a shuriken, you will be given a Defence number for your target. Roll two dice, and if the score is higher than the Defence number, you will have hit your target. The text will describe the damage done. You may find yourself in a position where you are unable to retrieve a shuriken once you have thrown it. Keep a running total in the box provided on your Character Sheet, crossing off a shuriken each time you lose one. If you have none left, you can no longer use this skill. You are free to carry as many as you find in your adventures.

ARROW CUTTING
Requiring excellent muscular co-ordination, hand and eye judgment and reflexes, this skill will enable you to knock aside, or even catch, missiles such as arrows or spears.

ACROBATICS
The ability to leap and jump using flips, cartwheels, etc, like a tumbler or gymnast.

IMMUNITY TO POISONS
This involves taking small doses of virulent poisons over long periods of time, slowly building up the body's resistance. This enables you to survive most poison attempts.

FEIGNING DEATH
Requiring long and arduous training, a ninja with this ability is able to slow down heart rate and metabolism through will power alone, thus appearing to be dead.

ESCAPOLOGY
A ninja with this skill is able to dislocate the joints of the body and to maximise the body's suppleness, allowing movement through small spaces, and escape from bonds and chains by slipping out of them.

POISON NEEDLES
Sometime known as Spitting Needles, with this skill you can place small darts, coated with a powerful poison that acts in the blood stream, onto your tongue. By curling the tongue into an 'O' shape and spitting or blowing, the dart can be propelled up to an effective range of about 15 feet. A useful surprise attack, the source of which is not always perceptible.

PICKING LOCKS, DETECTING AND DISARMING TRAPS
The ability to open locked doors, chests etc. With this skill you would carry various lockpicks in the pockets of your costume, including a small crowbar or jemmy. You are also trained to notice traps and to use the lock-picking tools to disarm them.

CLIMBING

Comprehensive training in the use of a grappling hook and hand and foot clamps, or cat's claws. The padded four-pronged hook has forty feet of rope attached to it. Used to hook over walls, niches etc, allowing you to pull yourself up the rope. The cat's claws are spiked clamps, worn over the palm of the hands and the instep of the feet, enabling you to embed your claws into a wall and climb straight up like a fly, and even to crawl across ceilings.

SPECIAL RULES FOR THIS BOOK

If you have not played and successfully completed Book 5: *WARBRINGER!* in the Way of the Tiger series then you begin this book with the equipment and skills listed. If you have successfully completed Book 5 then you should continue with the same character. Simply transfer all the information on your original Character Sheet to the one given here. You will carry five shuriken again, your flash powder will be replaced if you used it, and your Endurance and Inner Force will have been restored, though if you were tainted by the sorcery of an Amulet of Nullaq then you have a maximum of only 4 points of Inner Force. You also continue Book 6 with any special items you may have picked up in your journey. Do not forget to transfer all your Punch, Kick, etc., Modifiers to your new Character Sheet.

You may also have learnt just one of the following two superior skills, taught by the Grandmaster of the Dawn at the Temple of the Rock:

SHINREN

Also known as the Training of the Heart. ShinRen is a secret knowledge passed on during several weeks in the hills of the Island of Tranquil Dreams. You have learned iron control of your emotions; you can walk over glowing coals without turning a hair, endure heat, cold, wind, rain, hunger, thirst and pain that would send a normal person mad. Your instincts have been honed so that you may 'read' any person like an open book – having learnt the language that the body talks, understanding what people think by observing their mannerisms and the way they breathe, the roving of their eyes and their stance. You are able to understand a complicated situation at a glance and act, seizing any opening and taking any chance that appears.

YUBI-JUTSU
Also known as Nerve-Striking. You have learnt how to maim and kill with even quite light blows to vital nerve centres – a technique especially useful when beset by many adversaries at once, or against a formidable human foe. You know the anatomy of man in fine detail, the unprotected points and nerve centres where an accurate blow can stun or even kill.

When you are ready to begin the adventure, turn to **1**.

On the fifth day of Pantheos, Force-Lady Gwyneth asks for an audience which you gladly grant. She is even more ram-rod straight than usual, and her lips are pressed together in an expression of determination. 'A party has come from the Rift.'

'Glaivas? Doré?' you ask eagerly, but your hopes are dashed.

'No, we still lack news of them. The news that we have is all unlooked for. An enemy of the city has returned... a traitress.' She spits the word out with ill-concealed venom. Only one woman is hated by Gwyneth in this way – Foxglove, the beautiful courtesan who ran the Order of the Yellow Lotus, the secret informers of the reign of the demonic Usurper. You remind Gwyneth that there has been no proof forthcoming that Foxglove betrayed the city to Shadazar and the forces of evil from the Rift.

'What need of proof? Where was she when the Orcs and the Dark Elves and their Trolls overran the city? Gone. Disappeared – *poof!* – into thin air... Pah! Into the Bowels of Orb, more like. Now they are camped on the edges of our farmland, guarded by a hundred miserable quivering Orcs of the Severed Head.'

'They?' you enquire.

'Another woman is with her, a warrior woman, wearing a strange patchwork affair of scale mail. They demand amnesty from you before they will enter the city. They claim to bear news that you will find interesting.' You pause to think things over, but Gwyneth continues: 'I can take them with but twenty of my cavalry. Foxglove is no fighter. Then we will see what they have to say.'

Will you ride out with Gwyneth to try to take them prisoner (turn to **31**), proclaim an amnesty using the town crier, as Foxglove asks (turn to **41**), or try to use your ninja skills to capture them alone (turn to **51**)?

The tunnel curves gently for perhaps half a kilometre before you see any sign of another soul. The Torch of Lumen shows a small ill-favoured Orc walking towards you with head bowed down by the weight of a bundle of sticks. He shrinks to the side of the cavern to let you pass and then goes on his way. Turn to **52**.

3

You pour the antidote down her throat but it is several minutes before you see any signs of recovery. In fact she has been tricking you, waiting to gather her strength so that she can now twist away from you and shout out to the Orcs. Her lithe swiftness astounds you. Her sword appears in her hand as if by magic and you see it is rimed with frost. At last you recognise her. She is Cassandra, wanted by the priestesses of Illustra at Harith-si-the-Crow for the murder of their High Priestess, along with other dangerous worshippers of the insane god of chaos, Anarchil. You were attacked by three of them because you had slain their barbarian friend Olvar the Chaos Bringer in self-defence. Most clearly of all you remember that she is a breathtakingly swift swordswoman. You give battle, but the Orcs swarm over you, impeding you, and Cassandra is able to gain the upper hand.

Turn to **33**.

4

Passing a small alcove, the magician Eris's keen eyes catch sight of a strange samovar encrusted with large sapphires. It is about sixty centimetres tall and made of solid gold. He picks it up and examines it, marvelling at its beauty, but he can find no magic in it. It is passed from hand to hand, and you are invited to hold the priceless object. Will you decline and pass on by (turn to **164**) or take a look (turn to **64**)?

5

Gwyneth murmurs something about pneumonia and the running damp in the windowless tower that is the Palace donjon, but after a time she takes her leave and returns to her temple. You fall to pondering what to do about your poor friend Glaivas.

Turn to **393**.

6

The silver serpent-headed javelin catches your arm. Lose 4 Endurance. If you are still alive, the swordsman is now attacking. He thrusts at your heart and his sword is enchanted to find its mark magically. You try to block the blow. Your Defence is 6. If you are successful, turn to **26**. If you fail, turn to **46**.

7

The road winds gradually downhill, criss-crossing the canyon face in kilometre-wide zigzags. Every now and then it burrows into the rock, cutting through a spur that makes a natural archway of stone above the road. At the first there are signs of a deserted guard-post. If you wish to turn back and take the narrow path, turn to **287**. If not, turn to **307**.

8

Desperately you search for something small and slim to poke into your ear in an effort to dislodge the spider. In a flash you remember the jewelled pin. Whipping it out, you jab it gingerly into your ear and then pull it out again. On the sharp end is a small black and red spider, a miniature black widow. You wipe it off the pin on the side of the tunnel, squashing it. If you still have one of these tiny spiders inside your head, turn to **48**, otherwise turn to **52**.

9

The tunnel you are in is joined by several others and then winds down steadily into the depths of Orb. Soon you are down to the populous second tier. Here complete villages and towns exist, trading with one another, mining, and raiding each other for slaves and booty. You take a moment, just a moment, to rest and eat of the supplies you brought with you. After this point, you will have to start going even more carefully.

Countless tunnels diverge in all directions at this level. Finding your way, if you keep to the smaller tunnels, will be difficult. If you take the broader tunnels, you run a greater risk of being spotted. Will you try to find yourself a disguise so that you can bluff your way down to the lower tiers (turn to **299**) or rely on stealth (turn to **319**)?

10

If you have the skill of Acrobatics and wish to use it, turn to **30**. Otherwise turn to **50**.

11

You have hardly begun to fight when Cassandra's sword cuts at the back of your head. If you captured her sword outside the city, you lose 4 Endurance as her replacement sword is not magical. If she still has her Coldsword, the frost-rimed blade chills you to the marrow and burns in your wound. Lose 7 Endurance.

If you still live, it is a miracle that she did not strike your neck. Thaum reels away and Cassandra immediately puts an arm between the two of you. If you arrived here in the company of a band of adventurers, turn to **154**. If not, turn to **39**.

12

Lord Sile is a tough cavern-brawler and he reacts quickly to your kick, but its power batters through his block.

LORD SILE THE ORC CHIEFTAIN
Defence against Kwon's Flail: 5
Endurance: 18
Damage: 1 Die + 2

If you win, turn to **72**. Lord Sile leaps forwards and head-butts you. Your Defence is 7. If you survive the attack, will you use the Forked Lightning kick (turn to **362**), the Tiger's Paw chop (turn to **382**), Kwon's Flail, if you remember being taught this kick in a previous adventure (return to the top of this paragraph) or the Teeth of the Tiger throw (turn to **32**)?

13

You take her sword with you and cover her head with cloth to silence any ill-timed whispers. You carry her one step at a time out of the camp. Almost miraculously you succeed in carrying her prostrate form away while avoiding detection. You are a kilometre from the camp when she recovers enough to speak aloud. She says: 'We came close to killing you, Avenger, in the city of Harith-si-the-Crow. Why do you not kill me? We are sworn enemies.' Will you change your mind and administer a fatal dose of spiderfish venom (turn to **73**) or continue with her back to the city (turn to **38**)?

14

Thaum's fingers are making the strangest patterns in the air, and Cassandra and Tyutchev are looking at Foxglove. Foxglove calls Taflwr to her side to be her protector. He seems confused and glances between her and the enemy just as there is an eruption of coruscating light so bright it almost stuns you into immobility. You blink and realise that Cassandra and Tyutchev had expected it. They were not interested in Foxglove, merely anticipating the numbing flash that is the result of Thaum's sorcery. They are darting to the attack already. Tyutchev's black cloak seems to deepen the darkness around him. Cassandra, as ever, moves with the grace and speed of a panther. You are lucky you were not looking at Thaum, for you would surely have been stunned by the flash had you not averted your eyes. The four adventurers have not all been so lucky. Vespers reacted quickly enough to shield his eyes and Thybault too has not been stunned, but Eris the Magician and Taflwr are reeling back in a state of shock. Will you use a shuriken against Thaum, who is beginning another spell, if you have one (turn to **294**), or move aside so that you put Cassandra and Tyutchev between you and the master of illusion (turn to **374**)?

15

Foxglove's kiss has a strange effect on you. You find yourself gazing into her eyes and wondering how you could be taking such a noble and perfect person into grave peril. Rumours told in Irsmuncast say that Foxglove could seduce anyone, man or woman. You had imagined the tales to be a mix between fact and slander, but now you know the truth: Foxglove is an enchantress and you have almost fallen under her spell. The Training of the Heart that you learned on the far away Island of Tranquil Dreams is enough to stop you becoming her slave, but her enchantment is powerful. Seeing your reaction, she mounts the white horse, smiles and waves goodbye. 'Farewell, Avenger.' As she rides away you suffer a pang of anguish at losing her, but you are gladdened by the thought that she is out of danger. If you wish to ignore your training and call Foxglove back, heedless of her enchanting ways, turn to **75**. Otherwise you settle down, a solitary dark figure lit by the dying embers of the camp fire. Turn to **55**.

16

You tell them urgently that you are none other than the Overlord of Irsmuncast nigh Edge. As soon as you speak their attitude to you changes. While four figures approach, you go on to tell of Cassandra and of Foxglove, and of your quest to rescue Glaivas, your Ranger friend. If you have played Book 2: *ASSASSIN!* and defeated an Undead Warlord attacking a party of adventurers, turn to **78**. Otherwise read on.

You have a chance to look at them closely. The swordsman wears a grey surcoat with an unfurled scroll picked out in white thread across his chest. Your studies in the library at Irsmuncast tell you that this is the insignia of a reverencer of the god Gauss. The man in the white robe is a priest. He sports the cross of Avatar on his chest. The third man is in green, and is also a priest, though he wears chainmail, a worshipper of Illustra, Goddess of Life. The fourth, the magician, is a worshipper of a Chaos god. The five-spoked wheel insignia shows the Limitless Possibilities that may lead to good acts, however, rather than those that may lead to evil. He had been hovering in the air and now descends gently to the ground. If you have played Book 2: *ASSASSIN!* and killed a magician who carried a gleaming Sun-star Ring, turn to **352**. Otherwise read on.

They are good people, unless they are in disguise. If you

have the skill of ShinRen, turn to **278**. If not, they demand to know more so that they may judge your intentions. Will you trust them (turn to **298**) or use Poison Needles if you have that skill (turn to **318**)?

17

As you back away there is a crack when the chains that tether these monsters to their guard-post become taut, preventing them closing for combat. You may use your shuriken to force them aside so that you can continue down the roadway if you wish (turn to **77**) or, if you think this a waste, flee back to the lip of the chasm and try another way down (turn to **97**).

18

From somewhere beyond the chaos-bringers, a thin figure bursts into view and dashes to your side. You step back, but then recognise it to be Foxglove. She is in the most dishevelled state you have seen.

'Yes, run to your saviour,' says Cassandra with a cold smile. 'You've served your use. Now you can die alongside him.'

Foxglove gives you a pleading look. For some reason unknown to you, Cassandra must have been keeping her in squalor until you arrived. Turn to **74**.

19

Your throwing star catches the sister of Nullaq by surprise. She ducks too late, and it embeds itself in the crown of her forehead. She caws like a crow, drops a small bag and teeters to the lip of the ledge outside the store-houses. You follow up for the kill, but to your consternation she changes into a black crow and takes to the air, soon to be lost in the darkness of the chasm below. The green powder settles about you and begins to burn into your flesh like acid. Lose 4 Endurance. If you are still alive, you creep forwards to examine the bag that she dropped. Inside is a potion bottle, unharmed by the fall. It is pale blue in colour; one sniff confirms that it is an Elixir of Health. You can drink it at any time except during combat and it will restore your Endurance to its maximum score. Note it on your Character Sheet, and cross off your lost shuriken. You decide to take to the tunnels and move away from the edge of the cavern.

Turn to **9**.

20

If you have a shuriken left and wish to use it, turn to **100**. Otherwise you run to the attack.

Turn to **120**.

21

As soon as you have recovered from the battering you received at Cassandra's hands, you manage skilfully to slip your bonds and her grasp, and bound away down the scree slope in an avalanche of small stones. For all her quickness Cassandra is unable to catch you, encumbered in her heavy armour as she is. You escape and rejoin Gwyneth and her troops, who had been powerless to help you, unable to scale the pinnacle in time. You are preparing to press home an attack when, to your surprise, Cassandra and Foxglove, alone and undefended, walk up to you and surrender themselves. You order Cassandra to surrender her sword, which she does, reluctantly, and ride back to Irsmuncast.

Turn to **251**.

22

Make a note of how many times you attack the mage. As a magical heat crackles around his fists, you chop your own down at his neck.

THAUM
Defence against Tiger's Paw chop: 4
Endurance: 12
Damage: 1 Die − 1

If you hit him and have the skill of Yubi-Jutsu, or have reduced him to 2 Endurance or less, turn to **66**. If you have not succeeded after two attacks, turn to **11**. Otherwise, he strikes at you feebly, clearly out of his element. Your Defence against his burning fists is 9. If you are still alive, you may use the Winged Horse kick (turn to **47**) or the Tiger's Paw chop again (return to the top of this paragraph). You have no more time to use a throw.

23

It takes longer than you expected to reach the head of the valley. By the time you reach the encampment again, this time from the opposite direction, it is just past dawn and the leader of the war band, a Warrior Woman, is already at sword practise. It would be foolish to enter their camp during daylight, so you return to Irsmuncast. Time is running out. Will you declare an amnesty for Foxglove and her companion (turn to **41**) or ride out with Gwyneth to take them by force (turn to **31**)?

24

As you pass the samovar you experience a feeling of relief and a lightening of your spirits. Turn to **416**.

25

Gwyneth affects not to notice that you have had to apologise to her and leaves the Palace to go about her business as General of Irsmuncast. Now you will have to decide what to do about your friend Glaivas. If you leave Gwyneth behind at Irsmuncast while you travel to the Bowels of Orb, her position will become even more secure than the war has made it already. If you are trapped there, she is sure to try to crown herself Overlord of Irsmuncast. Turn to **393**.

26

There is a mighty clang as the sword bites into your iron sleeves and you are pushed backwards. The sword's descent is checked, however. You are gazing straight into the swordsman's face, which is contorted with effort. If you have played Book 2: *ASSASSIN!* and defeated an Undead Warlord attacking a party of adventurers, turn to **78**. If not, will you say that you mean them no harm (turn to **86**) or seize the initiative and attack again (turn to **238**)?

The gallery of caves is enormous. There are storerooms, mostly plundered, and a forge and an armoury, both deserted, but further down you can hear sounds of life. There is a certain amount of growling and wailing and much low chatter in guttural complaining voices. The sounds are familiar as those of a slum. Here the refuse, the helpless or foolishly scrupulous inhabitants of the Rift are forced to eke out their days. Here they are closest to the danger of crusaders, madmen like the Paladin Doré le Jeune, who come to the Bowels of Orb to attempt to slay evil beings indiscriminately, or to the many renegade orcish tribes who do not obey the Black Widow. You decide to take to the tunnels and descend to the next tier away from the chasm's edge.

If you were spotted on the roadway that leads down into the Rift, turn to **297**. Otherwise, turn to **277**. You only count as having been spotted if you were instructed to make a note on your Character Sheet.

The spider burrows deeper and deeper inside your ear. Desperately you shake your head and cuff yourself, hoping to dislodge it, but to no avail. Soon you can feel it fidgeting somewhere under your brain. It is a daughter of Nullaq. If you now have two of these daughters of Nullaq spiders inside your head, turn to **104**. If not, note that you are carrying a daughter of Nullaq and turn to **48**.

There is time to grease the hinges of the stone door before you ease it open and slip into the torchlit interior of the cavern-house. To your surprise it is richly furnished with ornaments and even paintings brought back by raiding parties. Seated with their backs to you beyond a stream that cuts across the room are two Dark Elves, one clad in the blue robe that denotes she is a sorcerer, the other clad in the green and red of a soldier. Nearby is a set of coffle chains as used to transport human slaves.

Will you steal the coffle chains (turn to **69**) or try to kill the two Dark Elves (turn to **89**)?

30
Leaping twice as high as the enormous Ogres, you perform a graceful triple somersault above their pikes. In their amazement the Ogres get their long weapons caught up, and you land nimbly and set off down the exit tunnel before they can move to stop you. Note that you have been spotted in the Sacred Vault and turn to **372**.

31
Acting on Gwyneth's advice you take only twenty of her best cavalry and ride out with them towards the point where the Orcs are encamped. They have chosen a reasonably defensible position in a narrow valley of one of the tributaries of the River of Beasts. They have thrown up earthworks on either side of the river at a narrow point between the steeply inclined walls of the valley. They can retreat up the valley if necessary, but the scree slopes on either side make attack or escape difficult. Will you ride around them to the tributary's source and then back down the valley behind them (turn to **81**) or waste no time and make a frontal assault (turn to **91**)?

32
Lord Sile, seasoned fighter though he is, is taken by surprise when you leap and clamp your feet on either side of his head, then wrench your body so that he falls sideways. You recover before he does and are able to give the killing blow before he can attack again. The laughter has barely died on the Orcs' lips before they are in full flight. You motion Foxglove forwards and continue on your way. Turn to **52**.

33
Cassandra throws you to the ground, where you are pinioned helplessly by foul-breathed Orcs. Two of them hold your head rigid, and she takes her frost-rimed sword and says: 'This is for my friend Olvar, whom you slew out of hand in

the Mountains of Vision.' She places the tip of the frost-rimed sword against the glowing green gem that you have instead of one of your eyes. Mercilessly she gouges the point into your face until the gem is prised free and you are wracked with agony. Sneering evilly, she pockets the gem. You will no longer be able to see invisible beings from other planes, and with only one eye your judgement of distance is impaired. Your Punch, Kick, and Throw Modifiers are reduced by 1 until you regain the Orb that was your eye. Turn to **273**.

34

The tapestry down one side of the hallway is ripped aside and torn to shreds by a colossal being. It is the Krathak, in shape like a chameleon, with huge pincers and claws and feeding tentacles around its cavernous maw. Everyone cries out in panic and begins to run, friend and foe alike.

The Krathak is not alone. There is a howdah behind its head; it is being driven by Dark Elves in red robes. These are the personal bodyguard of the Black Widow. It seems she has decided you shall venture no deeper than the fourth tier. You join the flight away from the monster to the far end of the hall. A hail of arrows discourages thoughts of taking a stand, but a bolas thrown by one of the Black Widow's bodyguards winds around your legs and knocks you to the floor.

You hear Cassandra shout, 'The Worldworm. It's our only chance.' Disentangling the twine of the bolas, you set off in pursuit of the others as the beast bears down on you. Tyutchev has reached the far end of the hall and is opening a large secret door. Like all seasoned campaigners, the chaos-bringers chose their ground well and have prepared a way of retreat. Turn to **411**.

35

Foxglove's kiss has a strange effect on you. You find yourself gazing into her eyes and wondering how you could be taking such a noble and perfect person into grave peril. It is rumoured in Irsmuncast that Foxglove could seduce anyone,

man or woman. You had imagined the tales to be a mix between fact and slander, but now you know the truth: Foxglove is an enchantress and you have fallen under her spell. She releases you from her embrace at last and asks you to keep her guard through the night. This you gladly agree to do, feeling you would do anything to protect her. She lies down on the other side of the camp fire with her back to you and settles down to sleep. You find yourself wishing you could embrace her once again. You would even lay down your life for her. Turn to **75**.

36

The two priests Thybault and Taflwr rush to intervene, placing themselves between you and the swordsman. Anger flares in his eyes and he looks to Foxglove for guidance. It is quite clear that his friends the priests will try to restrain him if he does violence to you. Foxglove, realising this in her quick, calculating way, says: 'Very well. If you wish to show mercy, I will gladly fall in with your wishes.' She suggests you travel in one party deeper into the Rift for safety.

As you go, you have a chance to listen to the group. The four adventurers are here in the Rift for a purpose, not merely to loot or to slay evil creatures. You have enemies in common. They are hunting three worshippers of the Chaos god Anarchil: Tyutchev, Thaum and Cassandra, the very people who seek your downfall. Thybault tells the story of how the evil three dared to venture into the great cathedral to Illustra and kill the powerful High Priestess before her own altar. Taflwr persuaded his friends to seek out and destroy the evil trio, whom they now suspect are somewhere on the fourth tier or below. Turn to **306**.

37

This is a difficult move against an axe-wielding opponent. The Dwarf-Troll's Defence is 7. If you are successful, it is knocked on to its back and you have time to dash beyond it and past the other Dwarf-Trolls. Turn to **197**. If you fail, the Dwarf-Troll catches you with its axe. Lose 5 Endurance. If you are still alive you decide to flee rather than risk your life needlessly. Turn to **97**.

38

A farmer at work in his fields greets you soon after dawn and is honoured to take both you and your prisoner back to the city in his ox-cart. You are waiting in your Throne Room for your prisoner to recover when a corporal of the Watch brings a message. General Gwyneth has ridden out with twenty shieldmaidens to meet the war band of Orcs who are marching towards the city. Not long afterwards Gwyneth presents herself bearing strange news.

'As we advanced towards the war band, the Orcs put Foxglove on a horse and poked its flanks with their spears. The horse bolted towards us, and they flung down their arms and ran. It seems they simply wished to deliver the traitress Foxglove into my hands. We let them go. Foxglove is being held in the Palace donjon.' You thank Gwyneth and issue an order for the two prisoners to be brought into the Throne Room. Turn to **201**.

39

You look to locate Tyutchev. In the second that your eyes are elsewhere, Cassandra produces a throwing knife and sends it flying towards your heart. It is only your quick reflexes that allow you to dodge the attack and backpedal to place the tall thief between you and the swordswoman. Tyutchev bears down on you like a thunderstorm, the dark and magical cloak he wears making it difficult to tell just how close he is. Now you must fight him. Will you use the Cobra Strike punch (turn to **181**), the Leaping Tiger kick (turn to **254**) or the Whirlpool throw (turn to **330**)?

40

You run quickly down the tunnel. The sister of Nullaq does not give chase. To your consternation she claps her hands and gives a repulsive laugh. There is another flare of fire behind you and a wall of flame has sealed her end of the tunnel. Will you run back through the solid wall of fire (turn to **60**) or run on (turn to **188**)?

41

Amnesty for Foxglove and for her retinue is proclaimed throughout Irsmuncast, and your unwelcome visitors enter the city. The Orcs of the Severed Head, plainly very nervous, camp on Caravan Field, and talk to no one; they are guarded by a special contingent of the Watch. Foxglove and her companion are escorted into your presence by Gwyneth and ten shieldmaidens. You are met with a double surprise. Turn to **61**.

42

The tunnel plunges downhill for a while and the cacophonous rumbling gets closer. Looking back, you see a team of Orcs in harness towing a wooden chariot with rusty iron wheels along the rails. On the chariot are a driver clad in an outlandish suit of spiked armour, with a polished brass horn seeming to grow out of his forehead, and an orcish chieftain – of all the hundreds of Orcs you have ever set eyes on, he is both the most brutishly strong and ugly-looking. By the side of the chariot lopes the wood carrier. He points and starts gabbling in orcish while the chieftain stares at Foxglove and grins unpleasantly. Will you stop and try to bluff your way past them (turn to **182**) or turn off the main tunnel into a side tunnel (turn to **202**)?

43

The poison does its work. Cassandra tries desperately to invoke the power of her god, Anarchil, Breaker of Edifices, but her tongue will not obey her. She dies and takes her secrets with her. Gwyneth and her troops had been powerless to help you, unable to scale the pinnacle in time, but now they reach your side. Seeing Cassandra defeated they immediately assault the camp. After the ensuing mêlée, you are surprised to see Foxglove's dead body alongside those of the Orcs, and you suspect Gwyneth's hatred for the woman of denying you the answers to the present riddle. You express your disapproval, but the deed is done, and together you ride back to Irsmuncast. Turn to **83**.

44

The samovar is indeed priceless, but you lose interest in it when a small spider leaps from its spout into your hair. Before you can stop it, the tiny spider has run across your face and entered your mouth, which is still open in fear and surprise. You try to catch it with your tongue and to spit it out, but it crawls up behind a flap of skin and then into your Eustachian tube. Before long you can feel the little spider fidgeting about underneath your brain. It is a daughter of Nullaq, the Supreme Queen who rules in Malicious Envy. If you now have two of these daughters of Nullaq inside your head, turn to **104**. If not, turn to **84**.

45

The battle is long and bloody. Gwyneth is a fine and strong swordswoman, and she knows all the tricks. You are badly wounded and have lost a lot of blood by the time she falls stricken to the ground. There was no quarter asked or given. In the end your superior martial skill and your Inner Force triumph over her weaponskill and armour. The word of what has happened spreads like wildfire. The shieldmaidens of Dama turn against you and are joined by those who worship the god Nemesis, Supreme Principle of Evil. Your position as Overlord becomes untenable. You are forced to relinquish the Sceptre, your badge of office, and with it your chance to save your friend Glaivas, the Ranger-Lord. You are an outcast and will die alone and unknown.

46

The sword bites into your flesh, and as it does so the swordsman utters a strange word, letting fall the scroll. It is as if the Hand of Retribution had struck you. You are battered to the floor. Lose 7 Endurance. If you are still alive, you have no option but to surrender, as the swordsman is astride you with two others, one in white, the other in green, flanking you. The magician hovers gently to the floor and now you can see all of them clearly.

If you have played Book 2: *ASSASSIN!* and defeated an Undead Warlord attacking a party of adventurers, turn to **78**. If not, and if Foxglove is with you, turn to **258**. Otherwise, you say that you mean them no harm: turn to **86**.

47

Make a note of how many times you attack the mage. He raises his hands before you and they burn with a magical heat. You twist and lash your foot at his side, avoiding the feeble defence.

THAUM
Defence against Winged Horse kick: 5
Endurance: 12
Damage: 1 Die − 1

If you hit him and have the skill of Yubi-Jutsu, or have reduced him to 2 Endurance or less, turn to **66**. If you have not succeeded after two attacks, turn to **11**. Otherwise, he strikes at you with his enchanted fists. Your Defence against this is 9. If you are still alive, you may use the Tiger's Paw chop (turn to **22**) or the Winged Horse kick again (return to the top of this paragraph). You have no more time to use a throw.

48

The spider moves occasionally, as if to remind you to live in fear, but nothing awful happens yet. There are no sounds of pursuit as you continue searching for the paths that lead ever deeper into the ground, but the sensation of being watched grows until your hair prickles with apprehension. Turn to **52**.

The shambler squeezes along the narrow tunnel, scuffing dried excrement as it goes. You realise it is heading for its lair, a low-ceilinged cave. Nimbly you creep up behind it and slip the wire of your garrotte around its thick neck. Within seconds you are gently lowering the shambler to the ground and stripping it of its grime-ridden furs. Using your skills as an impersonator you are able to mimic its shambling gait. Only someone looking at you closely would realise you were human. If you must now find a disguise for Foxglove, you decide to try the cavern-house. Turn to **29**. If Foxglove is not waiting for you, you resume your descent. Turn to **319**, but note first that you are disguised as a shambler.

The Ogres cross their pikes in front of each other, blocking your path, and you fall back a pace. The pike points scythe down at you, but you dodge nimbly only to feel the hand of one of the sorceresses at your shoulder. Her hand seems to sprout rods of iron that embed themselves in you, and then she has levitated your body off the floor so that you cannot knock her over. You struggle, but the pikes batter you until she lets you fall to the floor, a bloodied pulp. Your end has come in the eternal darkness far from home.

Night falls. There is a new moon and wind. Conditions are almost ideal for ninja. You are able to scout successfully without arousing suspicion. They have chosen a reasonably defensible position in a narrow valley of one of the tributaries of the River of Beasts. Earthworks have been thrown up on either side of the river at a narrow point between the steeply inclined walls of the valley. The scree slopes on either side will make silent movement difficult. Will you try to steal in over one of the earthworks (turn to **271**) or, if you are skilled in Climbing, get above their position and then down the scree slope (turn to **281**)? If you do not believe that either plan is suitable, you may circle around to the head of the valley and try to come at them from behind (turn to **23**) or return to Irsmuncast and ride out with Gwyneth and a company of shieldmaidens tomorrow (turn to **31**).

52

Soon you have left the second tier far above. For several hours you continue to descend without being challenged. The only thing of note which you pass on the way is the scene of a battle. Three Dark Elves and as many Orcs lie dead on a stone landing. One was killed while running away, but they seem to have been fighting on the same side. A scroll has been discarded nearby, its magic spent, but to your surprise you recognise it as a scroll that carries the blessings of Gauss, Enchanter of Arms, patron of sages, who took up the sword and fought on the side of good when the Pantheon descended to Orb itself to do battle, many thousands of years ago. There are no other clues as to who joined battle against your enemies the Dark Elves and the Orcs, but there is a vile and noisome gas lingering in the hallway which almost makes you vomit. Judging by the arc in which the bodies fell, they were attacked from a side passage. Will you take this passage (turn to **390**) or continue down the seemingly never-ending stairway (turn to **410**)?

53

Cassandra's sword buckles suddenly under the pressure as the Worldworm tries to snap its mouth closed. She falls and the Worldworm's jaws shut with an almighty crack, crushing you to death. You die far from home, deep in the eternal darkness.

54

'You see, Cassandra, I have done your bidding,' says Foxglove.

'Give me the Sceptre,' demands Cassandra.

You look sheepishly to Foxglove, but she dramatically throws herself towards you and says, 'You must, Avenger. They will slay me if you do not.'

"Then I will slay them first,' you cry gallantly.

Foxglove says nothing, but Thaum is beginning a spell. You decide to give battle, but if Foxglove is ever threatened note that you must always choose to protect her under any circumstances.

Turn to **74**.

55

At least without Foxglove by your side you can make full use of your stealth and agility. It is not long before you are nearing the northern end of the Rift. A war band of crooked misshapen creatures, their eyes to the ground as they shuffle across the stony fissured earth, causes you to lie low for a while, but when the creatures are safely past you approach the chasm. Note that Foxglove has become separated from you.

Turn to **165**.

56

If Foxglove is with you, turn to **96**. If not, turn to **116**.

57

This throw is well nigh impossible against an axe-wielding opponent of such girth and stature. You launch yourself feet first towards the head of the nearest Troll, but its half-dwarven ancestry gives it greater skill with the axe than you had expected. Before you can snap your feet against its ears it has struck between your legs, burying the axe-blade in as far as your stomach. Death is instantaneous.

58

The four are all men. They seem to be a party of adventurers. One in a grey surcoat with an unfurled scroll picked out in white upon it is a swordsman. A priest wears the white robe and red cross of Avatar, the Supreme Principle of Good, another priest the green robe and white cross of Avatar's consort, Illustra, Goddess of Life. The fourth is a magician sporting the five-spoked wheel on his robe, which indicates he worships Béatan the Free. This last is the man you killed while ferrying the Scrolls of Kettsuin back to the Temple of the Rock, whose Sun-star Ring you took but that you could not use. You do not know what means brought his recovery, but if he remembers the event at all he shows no sign of it. He is just as distracted as the rest of them by the chaos-bringers.

Their faces as they take in who they have stumbled across are quite comical. They line up for battle. There is fear in their faces, but this quickly turns to anger when Tyutchev speaks. 'I wonder that you dare to challenge us. You have not the power. Both Cassandra and I are more dangerous fighters than you, and you, fickle Eris, cannot rival Thaum's witchcraft.'

The priest in green begins to chant a blessing in the name of Illustra. 'So that still rankles, does it?' asks Thaum, trying to break his concentration.

Cassandra says: 'The High Priestess is dead. What is done cannot be undone. We have no vendetta against the followers of the Goddess of Life.'

'You who reverence Anarchil cannot keep an idea in your head for longer than a minute at a time,' says the other priest imperiously. 'But we do seek vengeance, against all who worship the insane god Anarchil.'

They are not even addressing you. You realise the rivalry of these people runs deep. Suddenly you notice the tapestry at one side of the room begin to ripple as if in a wind. Turn to **34**.

59

The sister of Nullaq ducks your throwing star just in time and it is lost in the distance – cross it off your Character Sheet. You follow up for the kill, but to your consternation she changes into a black crow and takes to the air, soon to be lost in the darkness of the chasm below. The green powder settles about you and begins to burn into your flesh like acid. Lose 4 Endurance. If you are still alive, you decide to take to the tunnels and move away from the edge of the cavern. Turn to **9**.

Too late you realise you have made the wrong decision. The wall of flame engulfs you and you burn like a torch. The brightest light of goodness in the eastern Manmarch has had its moment and now sputters and dies. The sister of Nullaq gathers up the ashes of your body to be used in an occult potion. The Black Widow has the Sceptre of Irsmuncast and your people will suffer defeat at her hands.

61

The first surprise is Foxglove. She wears the same peacock gown that she wore when you first met her and she petitioned to become a member of your Privy Council, but it is torn and travel-stained; the extravagant peacock tail train has been ripped off it long since. She is still beautiful, but her fragile beauty is that of the forlorn waif rather than the sophisticated courtesan you remember. The second surprise is the Warrior Woman. You recognise her haughtiness instantly. She is Cassandra, wanted by the priestesses of Illustra at Harith-si-the-Crow for the murder of their High Priestess, along with other dangerous worshippers of the insane god of chaos, Anarchil. You were attacked by three of them because you had slain their barbarian friend Olvar the Chaos Bringer in self-defence. Most clearly of all you remember that she is a breathtakingly swift swordswoman. Turn to **71**.

62

Round the curve of the tunnel comes a team of Orcs in harness towing a wooden chariot with rusty iron wheels along the rails. On the chariot are a driver clad in an outlandish suit of spiked armour, with a polished brass horn seeming to grow out of his forehead, and an orcish chieftain – of all the hundreds of Orcs you have ever set eyes on, he is both the most brutishly strong and ugly-looking. By the side of the chariot lopes the wood carrier. He points and starts gabbling in orcish while the chieftain stares at Foxglove and grins unpleasantly. You have heard enough orcish spoken by those inhabitants of Irsmuncast who are Orcs or half-breeds

to understand a few words as the chieftain calls his men to halt in front of you and then addresses you. 'Kneel, shambler, before Lord Sile of the second tier. Why trespassing far from the shambler hovels?'

Will you kneel and say that you are taking your slave to the third tier where you can sell her for a high price (turn to **82**) or remain standing and say that she is the Black Widow's favourite and that he and the Orcs had better leave you be (turn to **102**)?

63

When you are securely trussed, Cassandra, who has been measuring the gem against her own eye, returns to talk to you. 'I will say this only once, Avenger, so listen well. Your friend and trusted ally, Glaivas, the Ranger-Lord, has been taken prisoner by the Dark Elves in the Rift. Only one thing can save him. You must take the Sceptre that is your badge of rulership and surrender it to the Dark Elves inside the Rift. Then Glaivas will be released and you will both be allowed to go free. If you do not aid your friend in his hour of need, then you are no better than those who hold him prisoner in the everlasting darkness.' So saying, she orders the Orcs to half bury you in sand at the river's edge and then they depart, leaving you to struggle in your bonds.

A few hours later a party of shieldmaidens on horseback, scouts from your army, come across you as you struggle with the ropes that bind you. They are embarrassed to find you in such a helpless position but soon have you free and safely escorted back to the city. Another party of scouts returning at the same time report that Cassandra and the Orcs are returning to the Rift and that Foxglove is still with them. Note that Foxglove is Cassandra's prisoner. Now that you are back at Irsmuncast you must come to a decision quickly. Turn to **393**.

64

The samovar is indeed priceless, but you lose interest in it when a small spider leaps from its spout into your hair. Before you can stop it, the tiny spider has run across your face and entered your mouth, which is still open in fear and surprise. You try to catch it with your tongue and to spit it out, but it crawls up behind a flap of skin and then into your Eustachian tube. Before long you can feel the little spider fidgeting about underneath your brain. It is a daughter of Nullaq, the Supreme Queen who rules in Malicious Envy. If you now have two of these daughters of Nullaq inside your head, turn to **104**. If not, turn to **124**.

65

The silver serpent-headed javelin strikes the floor beside you and rolls harmlessly away, but now the swordsman is attacking. He thrusts at your heart and his sword is enchanted to find its mark magically. You try to block the blow. Your Defence is 6. If you are successful, turn to **26**. If you fail, turn to **46**.

66

Thaum staggers back, clearly near death, but you sense movement at your back. Quickly you grab him in a Whirlpool throw and pitch him into Cassandra, who had been about to strike at your head. She scowls, regains her balance and goes to tip a potion down Thaum's throat. If you arrived here in the company of a band of adventurers, turn to **154**. If not, turn to **39**.

67

Just as you turn to retrace your steps up the roadway there is the whir of a tomahawk flying through the air and a clatter as it strikes the side of the canyon nearby. You sprint away, stealing a look over your shoulder as you go – to see five Dwarf-Trolls, fat but powerful cross-breeds with pug-like faces, ranged across the road beneath the second archway. They are tethered there like dogs, chained to their guard-post; if you had walked on you would have been among them. They begin to howl, so you run on towards the lip of the Rift hoping to get out of sight before you are spotted by more intelligent foes.

Turn to **107**.

68

The first spider, which had lain dormant recently, becomes active again, and you feel them beginning to eat their way into your brain together. Suddenly you hear a voice booming inside your head. 'This is the voice of Nullaq, I who rule in Malicious Envy, Supreme Queen of all who follow the ways of malice. Know that my touch is poison and my speech petrifying.' With that you feel your will fading. The daughters of Nullaq have enabled the goddess to take over your mind. If Foxglove is with you, turn to **88**. If not, turn to **108**.

69

The hearing of Dark Elves is acute. As you deftly pick up the chains there is the faintest clink. Make a Fate roll. If Fate smiles on you, turn to **109**. If not, turn to **129**.

70

'To which deity do you wish to pray,' asks the sorceress. Will you say that you came to pray to the All-Mother, Fountain of All Life (turn to **130**), Nullaq, the Supreme Queen that rules in Malicious Envy (turn to **150**), Tanajla, the Guardian of Elvendom and patroness of women who practise magic (turn to **170**) or Zarahrayal the Temptress (turn to **190**)?

71

Cassandra strides towards the throne neglecting to bow, and General Gwyneth moves in front of her to protect you. 'I have important news for you, Overlord. Your friend Glaivas the Ranger-Lord is held prisoner by the Dark Elves in the Rift. Only you can save him, Avenger. If you do not yield the Sceptre that is the badge and instrument of your rule to the Bowels of Orb, your friend Glaivas will die the death of a thousand torments, a death so horrible that only the immortal Dark Elves have the patience to execute it. If you yield the Sceptre, then Glaivas will go free.' She pauses for your reaction. You ask of Doré, who had accompanied him, and she dismisses the question. 'If you care for the headstrong Paladin, find him yourself in the Rift.' Will you

ask her what she has to gain for placing herself in such danger while bringing you this message (turn to **186**), ask Foxglove whether Cassandra speaks the truth (turn to **333**) or threaten to hold Cassandra hostage against Glaivas's return (turn to **103**)?

72

Lord Sile lies moaning on the floor, giving his last breath. The Orcs turn tail and flee. Wasting no time, you hurry on down the tunnel. Turn to **52**.

73

The poison does its work. Your 'sworn enemy' tries desperately to invoke the power of the god Anarchil, but her tongue will not obey her. She dies and takes her secrets with her. You return to Irsmuncast where, later, your scouts inform you that Foxglove and the orcish war band have disappeared back into the Bowels of Orb. Turn to **83**.

74

Foxglove sinks to the floor. Her powers in such a situation are limited. Thaum's fingers are making the strangest patterns in the air, and Cassandra and Tyutchev are looking at Foxglove. Will you look at Foxglove too (turn to **114**) or keep your eyes fixed on Thaum (turn to **134**)?

75

In the morning Foxglove smiles at you and lights up your heart with joy. She asks for the Sceptre as a sign of your esteem for her. You have some misgivings about this, and struggle during the remainder of your travel to resist the temptation of falling in with her wishes. Lose a point of Inner Force from your current score. In the end, however, you decide to give in just as you near the edge of the gaping chasm that is the Rift. She smiles and in her eyes is the knowledge that you would do anything she asked you to. Having proved her point, she gives back the Sceptre and bids you lead on. Note that Foxglove is with you, and that she has enchanted you. Turn to **95**.

You become a whirlwind of motion, pressing the attack with all your strength and skill. However, you have known since you last faced the chaos-bringers that these enemies could match you blow for blow, and now Tyutchev and Cassandra attack you together. Faced with their practiced fury, you soon grant them their wish for revenge as their swords meet in your vitals. You have been slain far from home, in the eternal darkness.

It takes all your shuriken to force the Dwarf-Trolls aside, but your accuracy is impressive in hitting in the throat two that try to howl out the alarm. They cower and paw at their wounds as you stride past. You cannot retrieve your throwing stars from where they are embedded in the purple flesh of the Dwarf-Trolls, however; cross off all your shuriken from your Character Sheet. Turn to **197**.

These people are familiar. You take off your face coverings and greet them, to equal measures of surprise and relief. They are Eris the magician, Thybault and Taflwr, both priests, and Vespers, a swordsman. You saved them from a terrible predicament. They are dressed now as then. Vespers in a grey surcoat with an unfurled scroll picked out in white thread across his chest. Your studies in the library at Irsmuncast have since revealed that this is the insignia of a reverencer of the god Gauss. Thybault, dressed in his white robe with its red cross, is a worshipper of Avatar the One, Supreme Principle of Good, while Taflwr, whose robe is green with a white cross, reveres Illustra, Goddess of Life, consort to Avatar. Eris the magician, whom you remember as a strange, capricious fellow, is a little nervous at the sight of you. The five-spoked wheel on his robe indicates that he follows Béatan the Free. The five spokes are five of the ten arrows of Limitless Possibility that tend towards good rather than evil. You know and can trust these men. Now that they recognise you, they step forwards to embrace you in turn, hungry for news. You tell them much, and in return they pass on some useful information.

The four adventurers are here in the Rift for a purpose, not merely to loot or to slay evil creatures. You have enemies in common. They are hunting three worshippers of the Chaos god Anarchil: Tyutchev, Thaum and Cassandra, the very people who seek your downfall. Thybault tells the story of how the evil three dared to venture into the great cathedral to Illustra and kill the powerful High Priestess before her own altar. Taflwr persuaded his friends to seek out and destroy the evil trio, whom they now suspect are somewhere on the fourth tier or below. If Foxglove is with you, turn to **386**. If not, you may offer to join them if you wish (turn to **306**) or say 'May Fate smile on you', and go your own way (turn to **326**).

79

Fixing the grappling hook in a small crack, you gently pay out the rope and lower yourself in the twilight to a ledge below the roadway. Some way below, you can see the roadway crossing the face of the chasm again. It will take some time to reach it, but when you do there is no reason not to hope that you will be able to slip unnoticed across it and continue your downward climb. In the long slow hours of your laborious descent your ears become attuned to the faintest of noises in the dark air of the chasm. Every now and then you have to make a detour around a cave opening or ledge. The noises of flying things become louder and more frequent. Dark shadows wheel lazily through the twilit airs of the Rift. Then a cry rings out, echoing off the far side of the canyon kilometres away. An Orc has been plucked off the roadway by a great winged beast. Grimly determined, you continue.

Some minutes after the chilling cry, you see the black shadow of one of the huge winged beasts that carried off the poor Orc. It is a Demiveult, the name given to one of the forms taken by the Firedrakes, fierce reptilians that rule the lands to the north-east of the Inner Sea. A Demiveult is a huge winged reptile larger than any other Firedrake but unable to reproduce. The Dark Elves must have stolen and hatched some Firedrake eggs. They are able to hunt in the abysmal darkness by scent alone. The wings snap forwards and it begins to dive on you. You need two legs and an arm to cling on to the rock. Will you push yourself off the wall of sheer rock and let yourself fall into the bottomless dark (turn to **329**), throw your grappling hook around the beast (turn to **349**) or start climbing upwards and hope that it misses you (turn to **369**)?

80

Running on, you see, too late, a high recess in the roof of the tunnel. You are beneath it when you look up and a tiny spider drops on to your upturned face. You let Foxglove fall unceremoniously to the floor and slap at it. It runs into your hair and then into your ear, darting so quickly it cannot be stopped. If you have a Bullthrush Pin, turn to **302**. If not, turn to **342**.

81

Travel on horseback is faster than otherwise, but it still takes the best part of a day to skirt around and climb up to the head of the valley. As you approach the orcish encampment from the far side you realise it is hidden from view by the spur of a hill. A pinnacle of rock nearby, however, gives a good vantage point from which to spy out the land so you decide to climb it.

When you reach the top of the pinnacle you become aware that another had realised its value as a vantage point. The Warrior Woman who leads the orcish war band moves silently from behind a boulder, her sword, which glows coldly and is rimed with frost, pointing at your throat. You recognise her haughty bearing immediately. She is Cassandra, wanted by the priestesses of Illustra at Harith-si-the-Crow for the murder of their High Priestess, along with other dangerous worshippers of the insane god of chaos, Anarchil. You remember you were attacked by three of them because you had slain their barbarian friend Olvar the Chaos Bringer in self-defence. Cassandra is a breathtakingly swift swordswoman, and she attacks with the speed and balance of a panther. She has given you no time to use a throwing star. Will you use the Dragon's Tail throw (turn to **211**), the Cobra Strike punch (turn to **221**) or the Forked Lightning kick (turn to **231**)?

82

The chieftain sneers and scoffs. 'A shambler owning a beautiful human slave?' he laughs. 'So she just wandered into the Rift and asked you to care for her?' Again there is laughter. 'She looks tasty for a human.' He licks his lips while the Orcs slip out of the harness and begin to stride closer. Will you give them Foxglove and hope they let you go (turn to **122**), tell the chieftain that he can have Foxglove only if he beats you in single combat (turn to **142**) or attack them (turn to **162**)?

83

A month to the day of the war band's arrival Glaivas's body minus legs, arms and face is carried into Irsmuncast on the back of a hearse pulled by a blind carthorse. The hearse arrives undriven outside the Palace and the horse dies standing up in the shafts. There is no clue as to what exactly happened or whether Doré le Jeune shared this grisly fate, but the knowledge that went to the grave might have enabled you to save the life of your dear and faithful friend.

It might also have enabled you to save your own, for in the end your presence on the throne leaves you unaware of a plot growing against you until it is too late. One day you die in your private chambers, killed in a single sword thrust by an imposter who will now rule Irsmuncast in your name, bringing it to ruin. You have failed.

84

Every now and then the spider stirs as if to make certain that you are living in fear. There is nothing you can do to dislodge it now. You will have to carry on. Note that you are carrying a daughter of Nullaq and turn to **416**.

The amnesty is proclaimed throughout Irsmuncast, and your unwelcome visitors enter the city. The Orcs of the Severed Head, plainly very nervous, camp on Caravan Field, and talk to no one; they are guarded by a special contingent of the Watch. Foxglove and Cassandra are escorted into your presence by Gwyneth and ten shieldmaidens.

When Foxglove enters the Throne Room gracefully you realise she is wearing the same peacock gown that she wore when you first met her and she petitioned to become a member of your Privy Council, but it is torn and travel-stained, the extravagant peacock tail ripped off it long ago. She is still beautiful, but her fragile beauty is that of the forlorn waif rather than the sophisticated courtesan you remember. Turn to **71**.

As soon as you speak their attitude to you changes. They are still wary but not intent on killing you. You have a chance to look at them closely. The swordsman wears a grey surcoat with an unfurled scroll picked out in white thread across his chest. Your studies in the library at Irsmuncast tell you that this is the insignia of a reverencer of the god Gauss. The man in the white robe is a priest. He sports the cross of Avatar on his chest. The other, in green, is also a priest, though he wears chainmail, and is a worshipper of Illustra, Goddess of Life. The fourth, the magician, is a worshipper of a Chaos god. The five-spoked wheel insignia shows the Limitless Possibilities that may lead to good acts, however, rather than those that may lead to evil. If you have played Book 2: *ASSASSIN!* and killed a magician who carried a gleaming Sun-star Ring, turn to **352**. Otherwise read on.

It is unfortunate that you should come to violence with this group, for they are good people, unless they are in disguise. If you have the skill of ShinRen, turn to **278**. If not, they demand to know more so that they may judge your intentions. Will you trust them (turn to **298**), or use Poison Needles if you have that skill (turn to **318**)?

87

As you near the natural archway of stone your acute hearing picks up two sounds. One is the sound of rock on rock, the other the sound of metal on metal. If you are interested in the sound of rock on rock, turn to **127**. If you are interested in the sound of metal on metal, turn to **147**.

88

You had unceremoniously dumped the inert figure of Foxglove on the ground when the spider fell on to your face, but to your amazement she is now standing, a broad smile gracing her features. She has brought the Black Widow a far greater prize than the fabulous Sceptre of Irsmuncast. She has brought its ruler, Avenger, to be a slave and pawn in the goddess's struggle for dominion over the wills of the beings of Orb. The goddess could now turn you to stone with a thought. You cannot even deprive her of your life, for you cannot act for yourself. Your movements are controlled by the two tiny daughters of the goddess, and they will use your considerable powers to turn the world to malice.

89

If you have the skill of Poison Needles, turn to **189**. If you do not have this skill, you realise it will be impossible to surprise one without alerting the other. You will have to rely on your mastery of the martial arts, but who will you attack first? As you leap through the air, they turn towards you in shocked surprise. If you attack the soldier, turn to **209**. If you attack the sorceress, turn to **229**.

90

You surrender to them and one of the sorceresses puts her hand around your wrist. It sprouts iron rods that curve slowly round until they are like manacles around your wrist. You cannot resist as they take you away for questioning. If you have the skill of Escapology, turn to **110**. If you have not, there is no escape for you. They will torture you if you allow yourself to live, so you bite off your own tongue so that you bleed to death as any honourable ninja should.

91

You give the order to charge and the Orcs are almost taken by surprise. The uphill going is rocky and difficult, however, and your charge falters as some of the horses fall or go lame. If you have the skill of Picking Locks, Detecting and Disarming Traps, turn to **101**. If not, turn to **111**.

92

As soon as you take off the disguise Sile orders his Orcs to take you prisoner. You have no choice but to give battle. Turn to **162**.

93

Gwyneth and her troops had been powerless to help you, unable to scale the pinnacle in time, but now they reach your side and prepare to assault the camp. To your surprise, Foxglove, alone and undefended, walks up to you and surrenders herself. As you have her bound, a shieldmaiden retrieves Cassandra's dropped sword, and together you ride back to Irsmuncast. Turn to **251**.

94

You race to Foxglove's side and arrive before Cassandra's blade can fall. But to your dismay Foxglove grabs you so that you cannot defend yourself. Cassandra has never missed a stationary target, and her blade smashes your head. Foxglove has betrayed you for the last time, and you die far from home in the eternal darkness.

95

You reach the edge of the great chasm without glimpsing any of the Dark Elf magicians who might be on the lookout for you. The air is rank with the smells of sulphur and ammonia. Stale hot air seeps out of the great fissures that split the barren rock. There are no wild animals here at the edge of the Bowels of Orb, only dust. At the lip of the chasm you pause to look down. There is no bottom – or if there is it is lost in darkness kilometres below. To the east you can dimly see the other wall, towering a kilometre above you like a distant bank of cloud. There are many twisting stairways and tracks leading down the side of the canyon wall, and there is even a road, wide enough for carts and siege machines, winding snake-like into the depths of the earth. It must have been a terrible labour to haul up to the light the engines that attacked your city. Foxglove says that the road passes many concealed guard-posts. Will you take one of the twisting stairways (turn to **415**) or the road (turn to **7**)?

96

The tunnel you are in leads to a balcony above a great open underground plaza. In the plaza are rows of guruka trees, a cross between trees and mushrooms which flourish in large spaces underground, nourished by the bacteria and guano of bats and other creatures. They are like great still beasts, contorted into grotesque shapes and entwining as if they had been writhing together when the sun suddenly went out and they were robbed of movement. The plaza is lit so brightly by furnaces and blazing fires that your eyes, long accustomed only to torchlight, are dazzled. The plaza is busy. This is the main route from the third to the fourth tier, down the Fire Giants' Stair. There are no guards to be seen, just a steady bustle of people coming and going. At the far side of the plaza the largest tunnel and stairway you have ever seen lead down out of sight. Foxglove warns you not to attempt to descend the Fire Giants' Stair, for it is guarded at its half-way point by actual giants. They are blind, but folklore tells that the Fire Giants of the stair are gifted with sixth sense, that they can sense anyone who should not be on the stair and then they hurl flaming boulders and smash the trespassers under their iron clubs. In this way subjects who have no business leaving the lower tiers are kept down, just as interlopers are kept out. Foxglove implores you to search for the secret stairs that lead to the fourth tier. Will you take her advice (turn to **176**) or risk the stair (turn to **196**)?

97

The Dwarf-Trolls begin to howl in annoyance, giving the alarm. You sprint back up the roadway towards the lip of the chasm hoping to get out of sight before you are spotted by more intelligent foes. As you regain the lip you steal a quick look back. A figure stands beneath the first archway. A green and purple robe suggests that it may be a Dark Elf, perhaps even a sister of Nullaq. She shields her eyes against the light and is staring up at you. Note that you have been spotted on the roadway. You dart out of sight and take the nearest twisting stairway that winds down out of sight between two spurs.

Turn to **375**.

98

From somewhere beyond the chaos-bringers, a thin figure bursts into view and dashes to your side. You step back, but then recognise it to be Foxglove. She is in the most dishevelled state you have seen.

'Yes, run to your saviour,' says Cassandra with a cold smile. 'You've served your use. Now you can die alongside him.'

Foxglove gives you a pleading look. Cassandra must have been keeping her in squalour until you arrived for some reason unknown to you. Foxglove, whose powers in such a situation are limited, sinks to the floor and makes herself small, hoping that when the spells start to fly she will be overlooked.

Turn to **246**.

99

Though you are clad in your black ninja costume and move through the gloom as stealthily as a cat, many of the creatures have the advantage of living their whole lives lit by only the dimmest of light and one of them spots you, immediately raising the alarm. You have no choice but to retreat the way you came, as four Dark Elves riding flightless dragon-lizards charge after you and a dozen bows hum and twang. The shafts fall short, and soon you are nearing the guard-point of the Dwarf-Trolls once again. If you are skilled in Acrobatics, turn to **119**. If you do not have this skill, you must fight your way through (turn to **139**).

Even as you reach for a shuriken the twisted Dark Elf has spoken a spell. She thinks even faster than you do, but then she has two minds. Your fingers close around the star and you cry out in pain. The throwing star is white hot. You drop it to the floor as it turns to liquid iron. If you are carrying any other throwing stars about your person, they melt through your clothing and run down your loins. Lose 2 Endurance for every shuriken you were carrying to this point. If you are still alive, in a red mist of pain, you realise that they are all useless; cross off all your shuriken from your Character Sheet.

The sister of Nullaq has not tried to kill you in your moment of pain and helplessness. Instead she points to the tunnel ahead of you again. Will you enter the tunnel as she bids (turn to **40**) or try to leave by the other free entrance, guarded by two statues, behind you and to the left (turn to **220**)?

At the very last moment you realise that the earth before the defensive earthworks has been disturbed recently, and you rein in your horse and bellow out, 'Halt!' One or two of the horses plough on and fall down into pits filled with spikes which the Orcs have prepared under their leader, who is a woman in bizarre patchwork armour keeping them at the defences with the flat of her sword: the blade glows coldly and is rimed with frost. There is a flurry of arrows from the Orcs and three Warrior Women go down. Will you call off the attack (turn to **121**), charge again (turn to **131**) or dismount to press home the attack (turn to **141**)?

The charioteer Orc looks at Lord Sile and the team wait to hear what their Lord will make of this threat from the lips of a shambler from the hovels. Lord Sile seems at first nonplussed and then angry. A cunning smile creases his scrofulous face. 'The Black Widow entrusts her favourite to the care of a shambler from the hovels of the second tier?

You had both better wait in my dungeons until I can send a message to the Black Widow.' The Orcs slip out of their harness. Will you reveal that you are a human, not a shambler (turn to **92**), or say that you are a Dark Elf sorceress who has been cursed and turned into a mere shambler, but who has not lost her sorcerous powers (turn to **112**)?

103

Cassandra laughs and replies: 'What care the Dark Elves for Cassandra? I matter to them only as an instrument in their orchestration. Should I fail to play my part and return as they expect, they simply will proceed with their execution. No, you will have to take the Sceptre to the Bowels of Orb. If the love of a trusting friend means anything to you, Overlord, you must save Glaivas, the Ranger-Lord, or become no better than those who hold him prisoner in the everlasting dark.' Turn to **123**.

104

The first spider, which had lain dormant recently, becomes active again, and you feel them beginning to eat their way into your brain together. Suddenly you hear a voice booming inside your head. 'This is the voice of Nullaq, I who rule in Malicious Envy, Supreme Queen of all who follow the ways of malice. Know that my touch is poison and my speech petrifying.' With that you feel your will fading. The daughters of Nullaq have enabled the goddess to take over your mind. If Foxglove is with you, turn to **198**. If not, turn to **108**.

105

To take the Sceptre into the Bowels of Orb is to expose it and yourself to the gravest danger. Yet you remember how Glaivas has already indebted you to him many times over. If it were not for the warning of Glaivas that fateful day on the Island of Tranquil Dreams, your god Kwon would have been incarcerated in Inferno. Today you would probably not now be Overlord of the city, as he risked his life for you in battle against the Legion of the Sword of Doom. Your course is clear: you will risk all to save your friend.

You cannot ask another to share with you the dangers of the Rift. Foxglove must come with you as punishment for deserting her city in its time of need. She may be useful to you. But there is no point in taking an armed band. No matter how large, it would be outnumbered by the denizens of the Rift. Stealth will be your greatest asset. You take the Sceptre and swathe it in black cloth, then hide it inside your ninja costume. Leaving Gwyneth orders to publish the news that you are journeying to meet two saviours of the city, you prepare to set off to that darkest pit of evil, the Bowels of Orb. One other artefact you take from the royal armoury, the Torch of Lumen, an ebony rod topped by a cone of alabaster. When the alabaster is touched it gives off a constant light that will be invaluable in the eternal darkness of the Rift. It was enchanted by your father's most powerful sorcerer and looks to all but its bearer as an ordinary brazier.

If you have been injured, you can receive healing before you depart. Restore your Endurance to 20.

Turn to **145**.

106

You hope to minimise the interference of the potent mage and loop around your enemy. Tyutchev and Cassandra close on you simultaneously. Thybault and Vespers step bravely into the breach. They are skilled fighters. Thybault's flail whines as it whirls through the air and cracks as it smashes against Cassandra's armour. Her lightning riposte wounds the priest, but you are occupied with Tyutchev, who dares to attack both you and the swordsman Vespers together. He sends his bastard sword swinging at your head. The blade rings off of your iron sleeves but he redirects it flawlessly to deflect a thrust from Vespers. The next instant the blade is coming at you from the opposite direction. You parry again but find it difficult to counter attack, for the cloak he wears makes his position uncertain. You realise you cannot maintain this forever, and soon Thaum will turn the tables with his spellcraft unless you can disable him.

You must get beyond the swordfighters to reach Thaum. Will you use Acrobatics (turn to **161**), Poison Needles (turn to **257**), Climbing, if you still have your grappling hook and rope (turn to **279**) or, if you cannot or choose not to use these skills, force your way through Cassandra and Tyutchev (turn to **76**)?

107

You regain the top of the canyon before pursuers appear on the roadway below you, and take the nearest of the smaller twisting stairways; it winds down out of sight between two spurs. Turn to **375**.

108

The Black Widow has won a far greater prize than the fabulous Sceptre of Irsmuncast. She has won its ruler, Avenger, and he will be a slave and pawn in the goddess's struggle for dominion over the wills of the beings of Orb. The goddess could now turn you to stone with a thought. You cannot even deprive her of your life, for you cannot act for yourself. Your movements are controlled by the two tiny daughters of the goddess, and they will use your considerable powers to turn the world to malice.

109

Just as you pick up the chain the soldier begins to sing a haunting melody that is at once both foul and fair. Under cover of this distraction you retire to the door. If you already have the furs of a shambler, and Foxglove is waiting for you, you may take the disguise of a shambler while Foxglove takes the disguise of a slave (turn to **149**). Otherwise your only remaining choice is to kill the Dark Elves and take their clothes (turn to **169**).

110

If Foxglove was with you when you surrendered, turn to **290**. Otherwise turn to **310**.

111

Too late you realise that the earth before the defensive earthworks has been disturbed recently. The first wave of horses, including your magnificent white charger, ploughs onwards into the trap, a pit filled with spikes that kill many of your steeds. A volley of arrows from the Orcs kills several of the Warrior Women, and you hear Gwyneth giving the order to retreat. The Orcs swarm forwards from their earthworks, exhorted to victory with great gusto by the woman in bizarre patchwork armour. You are caught underneath your charger, and though not badly hurt you are helpless when, after throwing off several Orcs, you find the Warrior Woman's sword at your throat. The sword, rimed with frost, chills your blood. Turn to **151**.

112

Lord Sile looks a little uncomfortable. He is clearly unable to make up his mind, and his Orcs move no closer. 'Leave her with me while you return to the Black Widow and fetch a guard. There are many traitors and some Flatlanders in the third tier. You will not be safe.'

You decide to bluff. 'You would dare to defile the Black Widow's favourite?'

'I did not say so.' Lord Sile plainly has unsavoury desires and he now looks very uncomfortable.

'I shall report this to the Black Widow. You will all be punished,' you threaten. There are wails of terror and Sile is cursed by some of his Orcs. Suddenly the charioteer screams and buries his bronze horn in Lord Sile's neck. Sile bellows and wrestles with him to the floor. They are locked together.

The others join in or wait to see which side will win – Sile's supporters or those who wish for change – before they commit themselves. Sile's supporters are outnumbered, but Lord Sile's own strength is formidable. As you leave the battling Orcs, the charioteer screams again. You run for it. Turn to **52**.

Turn to **52**.

113

Cassandra is lying. Though to any other observer she would appear to speak candidly, you can tell by the way she is forcing herself to hold your searching gaze that she lies. It is true that she outbraves the lion; she risks everything by coming to Irsmuncast, walking into the lions' den, as it were, but she has slain lions before. She is lying when she says she is taking this chance for monetary reward. She lusts for your life to avenge the killing of her barbarian friend, and she stares at your emerald eye rather than your natural eye. She covets the emerald Orb that shines forth in your noble face. Turn to **123**.

114

There is an eruption of coruscating light so bright that it almost stuns you into immobility, but by averting your gaze you remain in control. You blink and realise that Cassandra and Tyutchev had expected it. They were not interested in Foxglove, merely anticipating the numbing flash that is the result of Thaum's sorcery. They are darting to the attack already. Tyutchev's black cloak seems to deepen the darkness around him. Cassandra, as ever, moves with the grace and speed of a panther. Thaum is beginning another spell. Will you throw a shuriken at him if you still have one (turn to **166**) or move aside so that you put Cassandra and Tyutchev between you and the master of illusion (turn to **174**)?

115

In the morning Foxglove is downcast to the point of abjection. She refuses even to look at you. If your heart softens and you give her the comforting she desires, turn to

305. If not, you will have to accept that much of your journey will pass in stony silence; note that Foxglove is with you and turn to **95**.

116

The tunnel you are in leads to a balcony above a great open underground plaza. In the plaza are rows of guruka trees, a cross between trees and mushrooms which flourish in large spaces underground, nourished by the bacteria and guano of bats and other creatures. They are like great still beasts, contorted into grotesque shapes and entwining as if they had been writhing together when the sun suddenly went out and they were robbed of movement. The plaza is lit so brightly by furnaces and blazing fires that your eyes, long accustomed only to torchlight, are dazzled. The plaza is busy. This is the main route from the third to the fourth tier, down the Fire Giants' Stair. There are no guards to be seen, just a steady bustle of people coming and going. At the far side of the plaza the largest tunnel and stairway you have ever seen lead down out of sight. Will you attempt to cross the plaza (turn to **196**) or attempt to find a back stairway down to the fourth tier (turn to **176**)?

117

You give ground but, instead of attacking you, your nearest assailant crushes Foxglove's head underfoot. Cross off any other notes about or effects involving Foxglove and note that she is dead. If you choose to cut your losses and flee, turn to **227**. If you choose to fight, you may continue backing away and use the Iron Fist punch on any assailant (turn to **17**) or charge in with a Leaping Tiger kick (turn to **37**) or the Teeth of the Tiger throw (turn to **57**).

Thaum mouths a spell and suddenly the air about his fists becomes as hot as a raging fire. This is all he has time to do, for with your first attack you leap at him and try to wrap your feet about his head, twisting to throw him to the ground.

THAUM
Defence against Teeth of the Tiger throw: 5
Endurance: 12
Damage: 1 Die − 1

If you succeed, for your second attack you may use the Tiger's Paw chop (turn to **22**) or the Winged Horse kick (turn to **47**) adding 2 to your Modifier and damage for this attack only. After this your other enemies will draw near.

If you have failed to throw him, he grabs at your legs and tries to sear your flesh. Your Defence against this is 8. If you are still alive, you may make a second attack of the Tiger's Paw chop (turn to **22**) or the Winged Horse kick (turn to **47**). After this your other enemies will draw near.

You rush straight at one of the Dwarf-Trolls, which strains at its leash to get at you, then you flip into a neat piked somersault and land behind the astonished beast. You are past the guard-post and you continue on up the road hoping to get back to the lip of the Rift and try to descend into the Rift along a less busy route. The cold-blooded dragon-lizards begin to slow and you escape. Note that you have been spotted on the roadway and turn to **375**.

As soon as you move, the twisted Dark Elf turns invisible. She did not move a muscle before disappearing. If you still have the emerald Orb in your eye, turn to **260**. If not, turn to **280**.

You decide that further bloodshed would serve no useful purpose and call off the attack. Gwyneth remonstrates with you, but you tell Foxglove that she shall have her amnesty and return to the city to await the arrival of her war band. Turn to **41**.

The chieftain beckons Foxglove to step up beside him on the chariot and forbids his Orcs to touch her. You let fall the coffle chain. If you are enchanted by Foxglove, turn to **262**. If you are not enchanted, turn to **282**.

'What part do you play in this, traitress?' Gwyneth asks of Foxglove.

'I am innocent of any dark design. When my own city closed its gates on me I fled to the Rift for succour and found only cruelty that surpasses understanding.'

Gwyneth becomes more angry than you have ever seen her. She is almost raving. 'Vile worm! You fled to those for whom you opened the city gate when we were under siege, but they had no further use for you. You are only of use in this city, Foxglove. You have no martial skill, no sorcery or priestly powers, only the low cunning of a poisonous gutter toad.'

You ask Gwyneth to calm herself and ask again why Foxglove is here. 'Against my will, Overlord. I am but a helpless pawn in an evil game.'

Cassandra says: 'I brought the woman Foxglove with me in order to gain safe entry to your city. I care not what you do with her, though I will take her back to the Rift as a token of what is to come, if you wish. Since you killed Shadazar, the

Black Widow rules the Dark Elves. Foxglove has made quite an impression on the Black Widow, haven't you, my beauty?' Foxglove throws herself to her knees and begs you not to send her back to the Bowels of Orb. General Gwyneth says that Foxglove is a traitress and should be put to the sword. Will you order that Foxglove be executed for the part Gwyneth says she played in the razing of your city (turn to **133**), send her back to the Rift with Cassandra in the hope that this may buy time for your friend Glaivas (turn to **143**), set her free on condition that she never enters the city again on pain of death (turn to **153**) or order Foxglove to be held, with the intent to force her to accompany you to the Rift after Cassandra departs (turn to **173**)?

133), send her back to the Rift with Cassandra in the hope that this may buy time for your friend Glaivas (turn to **143**), set her free on condition that she never enters the city again on pain of death (turn to **153**) or order Foxglove to be held, with the intent to force her to accompany you to the Rift after Cassandra departs (turn to **173**)?

124

The adventurers are appalled at what has happened. Thybault mutters darkly about losing your soul, and Taflwr suggests you attend an exorcism at the earliest opportunity. Neither he nor Thybault can perform one outside a temple, so you will have to continue in hope. Every now and then the spider stirs as if to make certain that you are living in fear. 'There is nothing to be done but to go on,' you say bravely.

Note that you are carrying a daughter of Nullaq and turn to **164**.

125

The Rift has been a cauldron of evil since time immemorial. All manner of wicked and unnatural creatures spawn there, giving rise to an endless stream of evil pouring from the dark chasm across the lands of men. Dark Elves, sisters of Nullaq, Orcs, Old Ones, Sons of Nil, Plague-Trolls, these are but a few of the denizens lurking in the unending darkness. The chasm itself is like an immense gorge surrounded by a honeycomb of natural tunnels and carven halls which stretch to the very centre of Orb. A man could walk for a lifetime in the Bowels of Orb and still not trace every catacomb and vault. You decide to make for the northern end of the Rift.

Turn to **165**.

You follow their gaze, and there is an eruption of coruscating light so bright it almost stuns you into immobility. You blink and realise that Cassandra and Tyutchev had expected it. They were not interested in Foxglove, merely anticipating the numbing flash that is the result of Thaum's sorcery. They are darting to the attack already. Tyutchev's black cloak seems to deepen the darkness around him. Cassandra, as ever, moves with the grace and speed of a panther. The four adventurers have not all been as lucky as you. Vespers reacted quickly enough to shield his eyes and Thybault too has not been stunned, but Eris the Magician and Taflwr are reeling back in a state of shock. Will you use a shuriken against Thaum, who is beginning another spell, if you have one (turn to **294**) or move aside so that you put Cassandra and Tyutchev between you and the master of illusion (turn to **314**)?

You look up to see a small shard of rock which has broken away from the wall of the canyon above tumbling down the rock-face to land on the roadway at your feet. At the same instant there is the whirr of a tomahawk flying through the air at you. You whirl around, but it is too late.

If you have the skill of Arrow Cutting and still have the emerald Orb in your eye, turn to **167**. If you lack either or both, turn to **187**.

Death is instantaneous. The swords descend faster than the eye can see, slicing neatly through the iron sleeves you have held aloft, through your arms and almost right through your body. The sister of Nullaq gathers up the pieces of your body to use in an occult potion. The Black Widow has the Sceptre of Irsmuncast and your people will suffer defeat at her hands.

The soldier is about to get up and sing when the sorceress lays her hand gently on his arm and touches a finger to his lips. They both hear the clinking of the chain and turn to attack you. The soldier comes first. If you have the skill of Poison Needles, turn to **269**. If not, you give battle to the soldier: turn to **209**.

130

Even the Ogres realise that you have made a mistake. 'Die, desecrator,' says one, and 'Speak not that name here,' raves the other. They order you killed. The pike points scythe down at you, but you dodge nimbly only to feel the hand of one of the sorceresses at your shoulder. Her hand seems to sprout rods of iron that embed themselves in you, and then she has levitated your body off the floor so that you cannot knock her over. You struggle, but the pikes batter you until she lets you fall to the floor, a bloodied pulp. Your end has come in the eternal darkness, far from home.

131

As soon as you have regrouped, you charge again, hoping to leap over the pit. Your white charger strains every nerve clearing the pit, only to fall foul of a net trap beyond it. Others fall on to the spikes, and once again the Orcs' arrows claim casualties. The Warrior Woman leads a charge from which those remaining on horseback can only retreat, while you are knocked senseless after falling from your horse and hitting your head on a rock. When you regain consciousness mere moments later it is to feel the Warrior Woman's sword at your neck. The frost-rimed blade chills your blood. Turn to **151**.

132

Seeing your success, Lord Sile bellows at his Orcs to stand aside. He dares to oppose you in single combat even though it has become plain that you are no shambler.

Lord Sile takes off his cloak to reveal a torso scored with ugly scars, the trophies of many battles. He stands before you, arms akimbo, like a wrestler. He is unusually tall for an Orc, as tall as you are. Will you use the Forked Lightning kick (turn to **362**), the Tiger's Paw chop (turn to **382**), Kwon's

Flail, if you remember being taught this kick in a previous adventure (turn to **12**) or the Teeth of the Tiger throw (turn to **32**)?

133
Gwyneth steps forwards and takes Foxglove's arm in a grip of iron. Foxglove screams in fear, but Gwyneth's face is set hard. She pulls the wailing woman out of your sight. The wails continue down the corridor and are then cut off abruptly. Gwyneth returns to the Throne Room alone. Note that Foxglove is dead. Turn to **163**.

134
Thaum's weird gesticulations are a wonder to behold. Just as you set out to attack him there is an eruption of coruscating light so bright that it stuns you into immobility. You blink and realise that Cassandra and Tyutchev had expected it. They were not interested in Foxglove, merely anticipating the numbing flash that is the result of Thaum's sorcery. They are darting to the attack already but you can only guess at their actions from the noises you hear, for you are temporarily blinded. You reel backwards, but the tempered steel of Tyutchev's and Cassandra's meet in your vitals. You have been slain far from home, in the eternal darkness.

135
The baying of wolves wakes you and, to your surprise, you see that Foxglove is up and standing not far from you. 'I'm so frightened, Avenger, I can hardly stop myself screaming out in panic.' Her voice sounds very shaky. Will you give her the comforting she desires (turn to **305**), go back to sleep (turn to **155**) or stay awake until dawn, when you can continue (turn to **115**)?

136
The tunnel you are in leads to a balcony above a great open underground plaza. In the plaza are rows of guruka trees, a cross between trees and mushrooms which flourish in large spaces underground, nourished by the bacteria and guano of

bats and other creatures. They are like great still beasts, contorted into grotesque shapes and entwining as if they had been writhing together when the sun suddenly went out and they were robbed of movement. The plaza is lit so brightly by furnaces and blazing fires that your eyes, long accustomed only to torchlight, are dazzled. The plaza is busy. This is the main route from the third to the fourth tier, down the Fire Giants' Stair. There are no guards to be seen, just a steady bustle of people coming and going. At the far side of the plaza the largest tunnel and stairway you have ever seen lead down out of sight. Foxglove warns you not to attempt to descend the Fire Giants' Stair, for it is guarded at its half-way point by actual giants. They are blind, but folklore tells that the Fire Giants of the stair are gifted with a sixth sense, that they can sense anyone who should not be on the stair and then they hurl flaming boulders and smash the trespassers under their iron clubs. In this way subjects who have no business leaving the lower tiers are kept down, just as interlopers are kept out.

Foxglove implores you all to search for the secret stairs that lead to the fourth tier. Will you take her advice (turn to **236**) or risk the stair (turn to **216**)?

137

This is a difficult move against an axe-wielding opponent. The Dwarf-Troll's Defence is 7. If you are successful, it is knocked on to its back and you have time to pick up Foxglove and move back out of range; turn to **177**. If you fail, the Dwarf-Troll catches you with its axe. Lose 5 Endurance and, if you are still alive, turn to **157**.

138

These people are the adventurers Eris, Thybault, Taflwr and Vespers. Their faces as they take in who they have stumbled across are quite comical. They line up for battle and you join them. There is fear in their faces, but this quickly turns to anger when Tyutchev speaks. 'I wonder that you dare to challenge us. You have not the power. Both Cassandra and I are more dangerous fighters than you, and you, fickle Eris, cannot rival Thaum's witchcraft.'

Taflwr begins to chant a blessing in the name of Illustra. 'So that still rankles, does it?' asks Thaum, trying to break his concentration.

Cassandra says: 'The High Priestess is dead. What is done cannot be undone. We have no vendetta against the followers of the Goddess of Life.'

'You who reverence Anarchil cannot keep an idea in your head for longer than a minute at a time,' says Thybault imperiously. 'But we do seek vengeance, against all who worship the insane god Anarchil.'

They are not even addressing you. You realise the rivalry of these people runs deep. Suddenly you notice the tapestry at one side of the room begin to ripple as if in a wind. Turn to **34**.

139

You will have to knock down at least one of the Dwarf-Trolls to forge past them and escape the jaws of the dragon-lizards, but you have time for only three well-timed blows before the dragon-lizards are upon you. You decide to attack one of them with a combination designed to floor him. Which three Way of the Tiger moves will you choose: a Forked Lightning kick, a Cobra Strike punch and a Dragon's Tail throw (turn to **159**), a Winged Horse kick, a Tiger's Paw chop and a Whirlpool throw (turn to **179**) or a Tiger's Paw chop followed by two Leaping Tiger kicks in quick succession (turn to **199**)?

140

Foxglove's robe makes the slightest of rustlings as she follows you, her dainty step in time with your own. If you were both spotted crossing the Sacred Vault on the second tier, turn to **240**. Otherwise, turn to **370**. You only count as having been spotted if you were instructed to make a note on your Character Sheet.

141

The shieldmaidens dismount, close ranks, and advance grimly behind their lozenge-shaped shields. On foot, battle-hardened veterans to a woman, they avoid the pit trap with ease and leap over the spikes to give battle. The Warrior Woman who commands the Orcs with great gusto exhorts them to fight, but they are no match for Gwyneth's troops. You see Foxglove clutching at her shoulder and whispering in her ear and, reluctantly, she gives the order to surrender. You decide to send the Orcs back to the Rift, cautioning them that if they are found abroad again they will be cut down mercilessly.

Turn to **201**.

142

The chariot driver cries: 'The shambler challenges the great Lord Sile, strongest of the strong, to combat.' There is tumultuous laughter and mock applause. Lord Sile takes off his cloak to reveal a torso crossed with ugly scars, the trophies of many battles. He stands before you, arms akimbo, like a wrestler. He is unusually tall for an Orc, as tall as you are. Will you use the Forked Lightning kick (turn to **362**), the Tiger's Paw chop (turn to **382**), Kwon's Flail, if you remember being taught this kick in a previous adventure (turn to **12**) or the Teeth of the Tiger throw (turn to **32**)?

143

You inform Foxglove that she will remain in the custody of the Warrior Woman Cassandra for the time being and say that you look to her to redeem herself in adversity if she may. Foxglove blenches and looks at you imploringly, but you keep your resolve despite the evil smile that darkens Cassandra's face. Note that Foxglove is Cassandra's prisoner. Turn to **163**.

Turn to **163**.

144

These people are familiar. You greet them. They are Eris the Magician, Thybault and Taflwr, both priests, and Vespers, a swordsman. You saved them from a terrible predicament. They are dressed now as then. Vespers in a grey surcoat with an unfurled scroll picked out in white upon it. Your studies in the library at Irsmuncast have since revealed that this is the insignia of a reverencer of the god Gauss. Thybault wears the white robe and red cross of Avatar, the Supreme Principle of Good. Taflwr the green robe and white cross of Avatar's consort, Illustra, Goddess of Life. Eris the Magician you remember as a strange capricious fellow. The five-spoked wheel on his robe indicates he worships Béatan the Free. These are good people. You know and can trust them.

Their faces as they take in who they have stumbled across are quite comical. They line up for battle and you join them. There is fear in their faces, but this quickly turns to anger when Tyutchev speaks. 'I wonder that you dare to challenge us. You have not the power. Both Cassandra and I are more dangerous fighters than you, and you, fickle Eris, cannot rival Thaum's witchcraft.'

Taflwr begins to chant a blessing in the name of Illustra. 'So that still rankles, does it?' asks Thaum, trying to break his concentration.

Cassandra says: 'The High Priestess is dead. What is done cannot be undone. We have no vendetta against the followers of the Goddess of Life.'

'You who reverence Anarchil cannot keep an idea in your head for longer than a minute at a time,' says Thybault imperiously. 'But we do seek vengeance, against all who worship the insane god Anarchil.'

They are not even addressing you. You realise the rivalry of these people runs deep. Suddenly you notice the tapestry at one side of the room begin to ripple as if in a wind. Turn to **34**.

The Rift has been a cauldron of evil since time immemorial. All manner of wicked and unnatural creatures spawn there, giving rise to an endless stream of evil pouring from the dark chasm across the lands of men. Dark Elves, sisters of Nullaq, Orcs, Old Ones, Sons of Nil, Plague-Trolls, these are but a few of the denizens lurking in the unending darkness. The chasm itself is like an immense gorge surrounded by a honeycomb of natural tunnels and carven halls which stretch to the very centre of Orb. A man could walk for a lifetime in the Bowels of Orb and still not trace every catacomb and vault. You decide to make for the northern end of the Rift.

Foxglove retrieves a few of her old clothes before you leave and you have to forbid her from packing an entire trousseau. She rides out behind you on a white mare which you hold on a leading rein, wearing scarlet and black, kept warm by a sable cloak. You leave the city under cover of darkness and camp the following evening, by which time Foxglove is complaining of exhaustion, though she has ridden and you have walked. You are not far from the River of Beasts. Will you stay up all night to make sure she does not escape (turn to **205**) or sleep soundly and trust to your alertness to wake you if anything is amiss (turn to **225**)?

146

Thaum's weird gesticulations are a wonder to behold. Just as you set out to attack him there is an eruption of coruscating light so bright that it stuns you into immobility. You blink and realise that Cassandra and Tyutchev had expected it. They were not interested in Foxglove, merely anticipating the numbing flash that is the result of Thaum's sorcery. You reel backwards, blinded and helpless, wondering whether your fellow adventurers have suffered the same fate. Your question is answered when Cassandra's sword slices into your midriff. If you captured her sword outside the city, you lose 4 Endurance as her replacement sword is not magical. If she still has her Coldsword, the frost-rimed blade chills you to the marrow and burns in your wound. Lose 7

Endurance. If you still live, you are fortunate in that Thybault's flail cracks against her armour and she is forced to step back, allowing you time to recover.

When you recover you quickly notice that the priest Taflwr and Eris the Magician have been stunned. Thaum is beginning another spell. Thybault stands between you and Cassandra, his flail thrumming as it whirls through the air. Will you use a shuriken against Thaum, who is beginning another spell, if you have one (turn to **294**) or move left so that you put Thybault and Cassandra between you and the master of illusion (turn to **314**)?

147

The scrape of metal on metal catches your attention. Instantly alert, you see an ugly pug-like visage staring at you from behind the archway of natural stone. The figure hurls a tomahawk at you with considerable skill, but you have time to duck as it whirs through the air and it clatters harmlessly against rock behind you. You drop to your haunches as a small boulder flies at your head. It shatters against the rock-face behind you. The sound of metal on metal that you heard was the faintest scraping of the chains that tether your assailants to the archway. Five Dwarf-Trolls, fat but powerful cross-breeds with pug-like faces, are ranged across the road beneath the second archway. They are tethered there like dogs, chained to their guard-post, but they lurch forwards with giant ungainly strides to assail you. Will you advance to the attack (turn to **207**) or flee (turn to **227**)?

148

The swords descend faster than the eye can see, grazing your chest then returning to their original position before you have time to think. If you passed between the statues, they would chop you in two. You have no choice but to leave through the tunnel indicated by the sister of Nullaq. As you cross the cavern once again she causes it to fill with a whirlwind of sharp flakes of copper which tear loose from the floor and bite into you. You lurch through the tunnel entrance. Lose 3 Endurance. If you are still alive, turn to **40**.

Foxglove is waiting for you still. She is probably quite lost already and must rely on you if she is ever to leave the Rift. She pulls back in alarm as she sees you shambling towards her clad in the shambler's furs, but when she hears your voice she breathes a sigh of relief. When you show her the chains, however, she is not pleased at the prospect of being treated like a slave. You reassure the pouting girl that it is merely to enable you both to descend deeper into the Bowels of Orb in safety. You fix the chains around her wrists and make her walk just in front of you, as if she were indeed your slave. Turn to **289**.

'Then pray, speak aloud the seventeenth rite of poisoning one's enemies,' commands one of the Elves. You did not even know of the existence of such a rite, of course. The Elves realise this only too well. They order you killed. The pike points scythe down at you, but you dodge nimbly only to feel the hand of one of the sorceresses at your shoulder. Her hand seems to sprout rods of iron that embed themselves in you, and then she has levitated your body off the floor so that you cannot knock her over. You struggle, but the pikes batter you until she lets you fall to the floor, a bloodied pulp. Your end has come in the eternal darkness, far from home.

Looking up into the exultant but cruel eyes of the Warrior Woman you recognise an old enemy. She is Cassandra, wanted by the priestesses of Illustra at Harith-si-the-Crow for the murder of their High Priestess, along with other dangerous worshippers of the insane god of chaos, Anarchil. You were attacked by three of them because you had slain their barbarian friend Olvar the Chaos Bringer in self-defence. Most clearly of all you remember that she is a breathtakingly swift swordswoman.

Gwyneth and the shieldmaidens can do nothing to help you now. You shout a command for them to return to Irsmuncast and look to the defence of the city. When they have gone, Cassandra knocks you to the ground once more where you are pinioned helplessly by foul-breathed Orcs. Two of them hold your head rigid as she takes her frost-rimed sword and says: 'This is for my friend Olvar whom you slew out of hand in the Mountains of Vision.' Then she places the tip of her sword against the glowing green gem you have inserted instead of one of your eyes. She gouges the sword point into your face until the gem is prised free and you are wracked with agony. Sneering evilly, she pockets the gem. You will no longer be able to see invisible beings from other planes, and with only one eye your judgement of distance is impaired. Your Punch, Kick, and Throw Modifiers are reduced by 1 until you regain the Orb that was your eye.

Turn to **273**.

152

Cassandra turns away from Foxglove. She was only trying to create an opening for Tyutchev. He is already striding to meet you and swings his bastard sword at your head in a single movement. The blade rings off of your iron sleeves and in an instant is coming at you from the opposite direction. You parry again but find it difficult to counter attack, for the cloak he wears makes his position uncertain. As Cassandra comes around his side, you realise you cannot maintain this forever, and soon Thaum will turn the tables with his spellcraft unless you can disable him.

You must get beyond the swordfighters to reach Thaum. Will you use Acrobatics (turn to **161**), Poison Needles (turn to **257**), Climbing, if you still have your grappling hook and rope (turn to **279**) or, if you cannot or choose not to use these skills, force your way through Cassandra and Tyutchev (turn to **76**)?

153

Foxglove leaves the Throne Room in indecent haste, and you order her an escort of shieldmaidens so that she may leave the city without being stoned. Gwyneth is plainly vexed, but you point out that Foxglove will not dare to return. 'Not until her intriguing has brought your downfall, at any rate,' says Gwyneth darkly. Note that Foxglove is exiled. Turn to **163**.

154

The battle has been going poorly for your companions. Thybault is wounded but is being tended by Taflwr, while Eris is still recovering from the blinding flash. Vespers struggles against Tyutchev, but the dark cloak he wears is imbued with a magic that makes it difficult to tell just how close he is. Vespers has not struck him once and soon will fall if you do not come to his aid.

In the second that your eyes are elsewhere, Cassandra produces a throwing knife and sends it flying towards your heart. It is only your quick reflexes that allow you to dodge the attack and rush to support Vespers. Tyutchev seems not to care that he now has to defend himself against both you and the swordsman Vespers; he seems more intent on killing you first. Will you use the Cobra Strike punch (turn to **334**), the Leaping Tiger kick (turn to **402**) or the Whirlpool throw (turn to **418**)?

155

Your awakening is rude indeed, for Foxglove's poison-tipped stiletto is buried in your vitals. If you have the skill of Immunity to Poisons, turn to **412**. If you do not, your last thought is the realisation that the Sceptre is now surrendered to whomever finds it and soon there will be a new tyrant of your fair city of Irsmuncast.

156

The tunnel you are in leads to a balcony above a great open underground plaza. In the plaza are rows of guruka trees, a cross between trees and mushrooms which flourish in large spaces underground, nourished by the bacteria and guano of bats and other creatures. They are like great still beasts, contorted into grotesque shapes and entwining as if they had been writhing together when the sun suddenly went out and they were robbed of movement. The plaza is lit so brightly by furnaces and blazing fires that your eyes, long accustomed only to torchlight, are dazzled. The plaza is busy. This is the main route from the third to the fourth tier, down the Fire Giants' Stair. There are no guards to be seen, just a steady bustle of people coming and going. At the far side of the plaza the largest tunnel and stairway you have ever seen lead down out of sight. Will you attempt to cross the plaza (turn to **216**) or attempt to find a back stairway down to the fourth tier (turn to **236**)?

157

The blow from the heavy axe has knocked you backwards. Foxglove is unprotected. Instead of attacking you, the nearest Dwarf-Troll crushes Foxglove's head underfoot. Cross off any other notes about or effects involving Foxglove and note that she is dead. If you choose to cut your losses and flee, turn to **227**. If you choose to fight, you may back away and use the Iron Fist punch on any assailant (turn to **17**) or charge in with another Leaping Tiger kick (turn to **37**) or the Teeth of the Tiger throw (turn to **57**).

158

Just before you strike the sister of Nullaq, she disappears. She has not turned invisible this time, she has teleported out of the cavern. You depart without a glance back. You may leave through the tunnel through which she entered the cavern (turn to **370**) or the tunnel that she indicated (turn to **188**).

159

In a blur of speed and motion you go into action. One mistake will mean your death as your foes close in on both sides. If you wish to change your mind and hurl yourself off the edge of the roadway into the bottomless darkness of the Rift, turn to **219**. Otherwise you are committed to this course. You stand off to deliver the first attack, giving the Dwarf-Troll no chance to hit you with its giant axe. The Forked Lightning kick is too subtle a move against this great beast, however, and it still stands after your double kick. The Cobra Strike punch doubles it up in agony as you hit cunningly just below the breastbone. If you have the skill of Yubi-Jutsu, turn to **239**. Otherwise your attack is doomed to failure as you slide beneath the bulk of the half-breed Troll and find that it is too heavy to trip using the Dragon's Tail throw.

Turn to **259**.

160

Leaving Foxglove to the clutches of the sister of Nullaq, you run quickly down the tunnel. The twisted Dark Elf does not give chase; instead she claps her hands and laughs. Perhaps it was Foxglove she wanted. There is another flare of fire behind you – a wall of flame has sealed her end of the tunnel. Will you run back through the solid wall of fire (turn to **60**) or run on (turn to **320**)?

161

You wait for the right moment then cartwheel away, avoiding another cut of the bastard sword by a hair's width. Your feet touch the ground for only an instant and you take to the air, soar out of reach of the swords of your enemies, land in a roll on their far side, and come up in front of Thaum, who hardly has the time to react. There are scant moments to cripple the spellcaster before one or more of the swordfighters are upon you.

Will you use the Tiger's Paw chop (turn to **22**), the Winged Horse kick (turn to **47**) or the Teeth of the Tiger throw (turn to **118**)?

162

Foxglove stands back and watches coolly as the Orcs assail you. Only three can attack you at a time in the tunnel, but the charioteer shoulders his way to the front and tries to gore you with his implanted bronze horn. If you have a shuriken left, you may cast it. At this range it cannot miss, but you will not be able to recover it. Cross it off your Character Sheet. Roll one die and take the result from your target's Endurance when you close to attack.

The Orcs carry long knives which they use like short stabbing swords to good effect. You decide against a throw in these quarters. Will you use the Iron Fist punch (turn to **355**) or the Winged Horse Kick (turn to **373**)?

163

You decide to try to find out more information. Will you ask Cassandra where in the Rift Glaivas is being held (turn to **183**), how many Dark Elves there are in the Rift (turn to **193**) or where her friends Tyutchev and Thaum are to be found (turn to **203**)?

164

At last the stairs stop in a great dimly lit hallway of dressed stone. A magnificent and sinister sight greets you. Away to the left is a huge archway, and beyond it a succession of carven thrones with statues of the former rulers of this part of the Bowels of Orb. In the shadows you can glimpse apparitions, the sight of which would freeze the blood of ordinary folk. To the right is a tall but very narrow tunnel, so narrow that it will admit only one abreast. Of the four adventurers, the one called Vespers the swordsman wishes to enter the Way of Thrones, and Eris the magician is already walking towards the archway. Will you advise them against this and persuade them to take the narrow way (turn to **204**) or walk with them through the archway (turn to **256**)?

165

You reach the edge of the great chasm without glimpsing any of the Dark Elf magicians who might be on the lookout for you. The air is rank with the smells of sulphur and ammonia. Stale hot air seeps out of the great fissures that split the barren rock. There are no wild animals here at the edge of the Bowels of Orb, only dust. At the lip of the chasm you pause to look down. There is no bottom – or if there is it is lost in darkness kilometres below. To the east you can dimly see the other wall, towering a kilometre above you like a distant bank of cloud. There are many twisting stairways and tracks leading down the side of the canyon wall, and there is even a road, wide enough for carts and siege machines, winding snake-like into the depths of the earth. It must have been a terrible labour to haul up to the light the engines that attacked your city. Will you take one of the twisting stairways (turn to **375**) or the road (turn to **395**)?

166

Your shuriken flashes across the hall and wounds Thaum in the shoulder. Roll one die and subtract the result from Thaum's Endurance of 12. He is no longer performing his incantations, but Tyutchev and Cassandra close on you simultaneously. In a flash a second shuriken appears in your hand and they both flinch momentarily. You somersault backwards out of range of their swords and hurl the shuriken. Tyutchev parries it, sending it shrieking across the hall into a tapestry, but falls to one knee as he does so. Cross the two shuriken from your Character Sheet.

You have gained a short respite from the onslaught and immediately seize upon it. You dive into a roll, passing to Tyutchev's side and coming up in front of Thaum, who hardly has the time to react. There are scant moments to cripple the spellcaster before one or more of the swordfighters are upon you. Will you use the Tiger's Paw chop (turn to **22**), the Winged Horse kick (turn to **47**) or the Teeth of the Tiger throw (turn to **118**)?

167

With a speed that defies belief, you sweep your arm across. There is the ring of metal on metal as your iron sleeves collide with the blade of the tomahawk and send it spinning harmlessly away into the depths of the chasm. You drop to your haunches as a small boulder flies at your head. It shatters against the rock-face behind you. The sound of metal on metal that you heard before was the faintest scraping of the chains that tether your assailants to the archway. Five Dwarf-Trolls, fat but powerful cross-breeds with pug-like faces, are ranged across the road beneath the second archway. They are tethered there like dogs, chained to their guard-post, but they lurch forwards with giant ungainly strides to assail you. Will you advance to the attack (turn to **207**) or flee (turn to **227**)?

168

The statues depict two beautiful Dark Elves. They are armed with slender adamantine scimitars, which are held up before their chests, and they face each other across the tunnel. Will you leap between them (turn to **128**) or cross the chamber and leave by the tunnel indicated by the sister of Nullaq (turn to **40**)? In either case you will be leaving Foxglove to her fate; cross off any other notes about or effects involving Foxglove and note that she has become separated from you. If instead you wish to pick Foxglove up and carry her out of the tunnel indicated by the twisted Dark Elf, turn to **180**.

169

The soldier rises and does a strange balletic dance to accompany his haunting refrain. The sorceress nods in time. Soon she will turn to look in your direction. If you have the skill of Poison Needles and wish to use it, turn to **189**. If, instead, you prefer to rely on your martial arts skill, who will you attack first, the soldier (turn to **209**) or the sorceress (turn to **229**)?

Even the Ogres realise that you have made a mistake. 'Die, desecrator,' says one, and 'Speak not that name here,' raves the other. They order you killed. The pike points scythe down at you, but you dodge nimbly only to feel the hand of one of the sorceresses at your shoulder. Her hand seems to sprout rods of iron that embed themselves in you, and then she has levitated your body off the floor so that you cannot knock her over. You struggle, but the pikes batter you until she lets you fall to the floor, a bloodied pulp. Your end has come in the eternal darkness, far from home.

Back at the encampment Cassandra throws you to the ground, where you are pinioned helplessly by foul-breathed Orcs. Two of them hold your head rigid as she takes her frost-rimed sword and says: 'This is for my friend Olvar, whom you slew out of hand in the Mountains of Vision.' She places the tip of her sword against the glowing green gem that you have instead of one of your eyes. Mercilessly she gouges the point into your face until the gem is prised free and you are wracked with agony. Sneering evilly, she pockets the gem. You will no longer be able to see invisible beings from other planes, and with only one eye your judgement of distance is impaired. Note that you have lost the emerald Orb. Your Punch, Kick, and Throw Modifiers are reduced by 1 until you regain the Orb that was your eye. Turn to **253**.

The echoing of your footsteps, no matter how stealthily you tread, returns from the faraway walls of the cavern. The feeling of being so far underground, surrounded by foes, is becoming overpoweringly unpleasant. The tension is unbearable; you feel trapped and vulnerable, and even begin to hear footsteps approaching that aren't there. When you are about half way across the vault, judging by the echoes, you realise that the footsteps are real and they are closing in on you from all sides. Suddenly there is a *whoosh* of flame and a ring of fires burst up ahead of you, then others to left

and right. The vault is like a huge underground temple. Mock pillars that no longer quite reach the ceiling cast shadows at irregular intervals. The approaching footsteps are those of a party of Orcs led by two Dark Elves in blue cloaks. They have been walking towards the glow of the Torch of Lumen, but now they can see you in the light of the fires. The chase is on. Ahead of you, thirty metres away, is a gallery leading to stairs, but it is guarded by a score of Orcs with crossbows. To the right, fifteen metres away, is another tunnel, but this is guarded by two Ogres wearing leather armour and wielding four-metre-long pikes like the men of Antiochis used to in the golden age of the Inner Sea. To the left of you, about twelve metres away, are the Elves and Orcs. Will you run towards the Ogres (turn to **192**) or the gallery (turn to **212**) or stop where you are (turn to **232**)?

173
Gwyneth escorts Foxglove none too gently to the donjon, the windowless tower at the north-east corner of the Palace. There she will languish until you finish your business with the Warrior Woman.

You decide to try to find out more information. Will you ask Cassandra where in the Rift Glaivas is being held (turn to **215**), how many Dark Elves there are in the Rift (turn to **235**) or where her friends Tyutchev and Thaum are to be found (turn to **255**)?

174
As you move, so does Cassandra – not towards you but towards Foxglove, who is cowering as far away as she can. Cassandra's sword is raised, ready to strike. If you want to protect Foxglove, turn to **94**. If, instead, you attack Tyutchev, who is running at you, turn to **152**.

175
The Dark Elf holds his sword level before you and in the light it shines with poison. Trusting in your ability to deflect it with your iron sleeves, you drive your fist towards his face.

DARK ELF SURVIVOR
Defence against Iron Fist punch: 6
Endurance: 10
Damage: 2 Dice *
* Damage is 1 Die if you have Immunity to Poisons

If you have killed him, turn to **263**. Otherwise, he spins his sword around and slashes at your throat. Your Defence is 8. If you are still alive, you may use the Forked Lightning kick (turn to **185**), the Dragon's Tail throw (turn to **195**) or the Iron Fist punch again (return to the top of this paragraph).

176

It takes more than a day to find an alternative to the Fire Giants' Stair. Meanwhile you eat food that you steal from the wicked denizens of the Rift and take what sleep you can. In the end, only by covertly watching the thieves of the twilit world, mainly Elves and Orcs who have their own thieves' cant – unlike any language you have heard – do you discover a secret doorway in a rock-face. It takes a little while to discover how the mechanism works, but at last you swing the rock aside and begin the descent. Turn to **296**.

177

Foxglove is already coming round as you pick her up. You flee just in time. The Dwarf-Trolls' chains snap taut just before they catch you and they begin to howl in annoyance, giving the alarm. Foxglove pulls a phial from a pleat in her boot and drinks it – a healing potion. Soon she is fully restored and can run unaided. You sprint back up the roadway towards the lip of the chasm, hoping to get out of sight before you are spotted by more intelligent foes. As you regain the lip you steal a quick look back. A figure stands beneath the first archway. A green and purple robe suggests it may be a Dark Elf, perhaps even a sister of Nullaq. She shields her eyes against the light and is staring up at you. Note that you have been spotted on the roadway. You dart out of sight and take the nearest twisting stairway that winds down out of sight between two spurs. Turn to **415**.

178

You hope to minimise the interference of the potent mage and loop around your enemy. Tyutchev strides purposefully to meet you, swinging his bastard sword at your head in a single movement. The blade rings off of your iron sleeves and in an instant is coming at you from the opposite direction. You parry again but find it difficult to counter attack, for the cloak he wears makes his position uncertain. As Cassandra comes around his side, you realise you cannot maintain this forever, and soon Thaum will turn the tables with his spellcraft unless you can disable him.

You must get beyond the swordfighters to reach Thaum. Will you use Acrobatics (turn to **161**), Poison Needles (turn to **257**), Climbing, if you still have your grappling hook and rope (turn to **279**) or, if you cannot or choose not to use these skills, force your way through Cassandra and Tyutchev (turn to **76**)?

179

In a blur of speed and motion you go into action. One mistake will mean your death as your foes close in on both sides. If you wish to change your mind and hurl yourself off the edge of the roadway into the bottomless darkness of the Rift, turn to **219**. Otherwise you are committed to this course. You stand off to deliver the first attack, the Winged Horse kick, giving the Dwarf-Troll no time to hit you with its giant axe. It is knocked to its knees by the power of your blow. You follow up with a Tiger's Paw chop, knocking it off balance as it tries to regain its feet, causing it to drop the axe with a crash. You then step in to put the heavy beast on its back with a Whirlpool throw before it can regain its balance. You are soon past the guard-post and you continue on up the road hoping to get back to the lip of the Rift and try to descend into the Rift along a less busy route. The cold-blooded dragon-lizards begin to slow down and you escape. Note on your character sheet that you have been spotted on the roadway and then turn to **375**.

180

The sister of Nullaq allows you to pick up Foxglove's slack body and watches calmly while you carry her to the tunnel. She does not give chase. Instead she claps her hands and gives a repulsive laugh. There is another flare of fire behind you and a wall of flame has sealed her end of the tunnel. Will you run back through the solid wall of fire (turn to **60**) or run on (turn to **80**)?

181

Make a note of how many times you attack the thief. Tyutchev grins evilly as he moves in to the attack. His enormous bastard sword swirls through the air faster than you might have believed possible and you can only hope to strike even faster. If your attack succeeds and you have the skill of Yubi-Jutsu, you may add 2 to the damage, but you may not combine Nerve-Striking with Inner Force.

TYUTCHEV
Defence against Cobra Strike punch: 8
Endurance: 20
Damage: 2 Dice + 2

If you hit him and reduce him to 3 Endurance or less, turn to **208**. If you have not succeeded after three attacks, turn to **396**. Otherwise, Tyutchev's blade arcs in a backwards swing up underneath your outstretched arm. Your Defence is 8. If you are still alive, use the Leaping Tiger kick (turn to **254**), the Whirlpool throw (turn to **330**) or the Cobra Strike punch again (return to the top of this paragraph).

182

The Orcs halt the chariot before you and the chieftain speaks. 'Kneel, shambler, before Lord Sile of the second tier. Why trespassing so far from the shambler hovels?' Will you kneel and say that you are taking your slave to the third tier where you can sell her for a high price (turn to **82**) or remain standing and say that she is the Black Widow's favourite and that he and the Orcs had better leave you be (turn to **102**)?

183

'Glaivas is kept captive beyond the seventh tier in the area known as the Forbidden Sanctuary. The Black Widow's web reaches out from the hub there.' You ask Cassandra one more question. Will you ask how many Dark Elves there are in the Rift (turn to **213**) or where her friends Tyutchev and Thaum are to be found (turn to **223**)?

184

The narrow way continues in a straight line for many hundreds of metres without opening out or offering any openings. Towards its end it climbs slightly, and when you are half way up the incline the floor tilts suddenly and pitches you forwards on to your face in a small well-lit room hung with lush tapestries. When you stand and look around, you receive something of a shock. Turn to **224**.

185

The wounded Dark Elf is still elegant in motion. To get past his defence, you feint with a kick at the side of his knee and then strike again right under his ribs when he lowers his sword.

DARK ELF SURVIVOR
Defence against Forked Lightning kick: 7
Endurance: 10
Damage: 2 Dice *
* Damage is 1 Die if you have Immunity to Poisons

If you have killed him, turn to **263**. Otherwise, he raises his envenomed blade immediately and slashes at your stomach. Your Defence is 7. If you are still alive, you may use the Iron Fist punch (turn to **175**), the Dragon's Tail throw (turn to **195**) or the Forked Lightning kick again (return to the top of this paragraph).

186

Cassandra replies that she has been promised riches beyond man's wildest dreams and that danger to her is nothing for she outbraves the lion. If you have the skill of ShinRen, turn to **113**. Otherwise turn to **123**.

187

You try to duck but you are too late. The tomahawk embeds itself in your side with such force that you are knocked to your knees. Lose 7 Endurance. If you still live, you drop prone as a small boulder flies at your head. It shatters against the rock-face behind you. The sound of metal on metal that you heard was the faintest scraping of the chains that tether your assailants to the archway. Five Dwarf-Trolls, fat but powerful cross-breeds with pug-like faces, are ranged across the road beneath the second archway. They are tethered there like dogs, chained to their guard-post, but they lurch forwards with giant ungainly strides to assail you. You struggle to your feet, but not before the first is upon you. Turn to **247**.

188

Running on you see, too late, a high recess in the roof of the tunnel. You are beneath it when you look up and a tiny spider drops on to your upturned face. You slap at it, but it runs into your hair and then into your ear, darting so quickly that it cannot be stopped. If you have a Bullthrush Pin, turn to **8**. If not, turn to **28**.

189

Just as the sorceress spies you and her eyes widen in alarm, so the poison needle hits her cheek. The soldier whirls around suddenly to face you as she slumps to the floor just in time for your second needle to bury itself in his lip. They die swiftly, and you gather their robes, belts and sandals plus two hoods that you find in a box. There is also a small jewelled pin, with a golden bullthrush for a head, inside an ivory box. Note that you have the Bullthrush Pin. If Foxglove is not with you, donning the green and red robe should be all the disguise you need, so you leave the other as well as the coffle chains you located earlier. Note your disguise and turn to **289**. If Foxglove is waiting, turn to **249**.

The Elves begin to mock you. 'A slave to the Temptress, eh? You will not find her ear here, nor any other part of her, come to that.' The Orcs snigger unpleasantly. 'Begone! Slink back to the fourth tier where you belong.' The sorceress points to the gallery, and you waste no time doing as she says. Soon you have left the Sacred Vault behind. Turn to **372**.

Cassandra has defeated you, but her final blow, which should have killed you, is pulled at the last moment. She has spared your life. Her sword is at your throat; its frost-rimed blade chills your blood as she ties your hands together behind your back. Then she pulls you down the scree slope from the pinnacle towards where her Orcs are encamped. If you have the skill of Escapology, turn to **21**. If not, turn to **171**.

The Dark Elves speak a command in their lilting language when you are six metres from the Ogres. If Foxglove is with you, turn to **392**. If not, turn to **10**.

'More than even you can hope to elude, Avenger,' responds the Warrior Woman glibly. You ask Cassandra one more question. Will you ask her where in the Rift Glaivas is being held (turn to **233**) or where her friends Tyutchev and Thaum are to be found (turn to **223**)?

You follow their gaze, and there is an eruption of coruscating light so bright it almost stuns you into immobility. You blink and realise that Cassandra and Tyutchev had expected it. They were not interested in the tapestry, merely anticipating the numbing flash that is the result of Thaum's sorcery. They are darting to the attack already. Tyutchev's black cloak seems to deepen the darkness around him. Cassandra, as ever, moves with the grace and speed of a panther. The four adventurers have not all been as lucky as you. Vespers reacted quickly enough to shield his eyes and Thybault too has not been stunned, but Eris the Magician and Taflwr are reeling back in a state of shock. Will you use a shuriken against Thaum, who is beginning another spell, if you have one (turn to **294**) or move aside so that you put Cassandra and Tyutchev between you and the master of illusion (turn to **106**)?

195

Even more nimble than the elf, you dive to the ground and wrap your legs around his, seeking to topple him to the stone floor.

DARK ELF SURVIVOR
Defence against Dragon's Tail throw: 6
Endurance: 10
Damage: 2 Dice *
* Damage is 1 Die if you have Immunity to Poisons

If you succeed, he goes falling as his sword cuts the air above. You continue your spin and get your legs under you. Now you may follow up as he tries to regain his feet with the Iron Fist punch (turn to **175**) or the Forked Lightning kick (turn to **185**), adding 2 to your Modifier and damage for this attack only.

If you fail, the Dark Elf turns his blade down on you and tries to bury it in your gut. The entire length is poisoned. Your Defence is 7. If you survive, you may use the Iron Fist punch (turn to **175**) or the Forked Lightning kick (turn to **185**).

196

Oddly enough your stealth while crossing the plaza appears to be wasted. Two Dark Elves moving silently from behind a guruka tree come face to face with you by accident, but they do not even seem to register your presence. By the time you near the stairway there is quite a press of people around you,

but none of them seems about to raise the alarm or even speak. They stream down the twelve-metre-wide stairway which glows redly, like the stairway to hell, in the light of banks of fires on either side. Half way down are what look like perfect waxwork models of six Fire Giants, their dark hirsute bodies glowing in the rubescent firelight. They are as still as statues and no one even looks at them. Will you turn back (turn to **376**) or continue (turn to **336**)?

197

The Dwarf-Trolls make no effort to give the alarm now. Perhaps they will suffer if it becomes known that you succeeded in passing them at the guard-post. The road winds on ever further down into the twilit realm of the Rift. There is a tunnel leading off into the rock. Will you take it (turn to **217**) or continue on the roadway around the next corner (turn to **237**)?

198

Foxglove stands before you, a broad smile gracing her features. She has brought the Black Widow a far greater prize than the fabulous Sceptre of Irsmuncast. She has brought its ruler, Avenger, to be a slave and pawn in the goddess's struggle for dominion over the wills of the beings of Orb. The goddess could now turn you to stone with a thought. You cannot even deprive her of your life, for you cannot act for yourself. Your movements are controlled by the two tiny daughters of the goddess, and they will use your considerable powers to turn the world to malice.

199

In a blur of speed and motion you go into action. One mistake will mean your death as your foes close in on both sides. If you wish to change your mind and hurl yourself off the edge of the roadway into the bottomless darkness of the Rift, turn to **219**. Otherwise you are committed to this course. You have to step close to deliver the first attack, allowing the Dwarf-Troll to swing its giant axe at your head. Your Defence is 7. If you are hit, you are knocked to the ground; turn to **259**. Otherwise your blow causes the beast to double up in pain. If you have the skill of Yubi-Jutsu, turn to **239**. If not, you launch yourself into a Leaping Tiger kick. You have two attempts to knock the Dwarf-Troll to the ground. Its Defence is 8. If you fail, you are in turn knocked to the ground by one of the other Dwarf-Trolls; turn to **259**. If you succeed, you jump over the stricken body and are past the guard-post. You continue on up the road hoping to get back to the lip of the Rift and try to descend into the Rift along a less busy route. The cold-blooded dragon-lizards begin to slow down and you escape. Note that you have been spotted on the roadway and turn to **375**.

200

If you have been enchanted by Foxglove, turn to **380**. If not, cross off any other notes about or effects involving Foxglove and note that she has become separated from you. Turn to **20**.

201

Later that day the prisoners are brought before you in the Throne Room at Irsmuncast and you are met with a double surprise. The first surprise is Foxglove. She wears the same peacock gown that had looked so stunning when you first met her and she petitioned to become a member of your Privy Council, but it is torn and travel-stained. The extravagant peacock tail train has been ripped off it long since. She is still beautiful, but her fragile beauty is that of the forlorn waif rather than the sophisticated courtesan. The second surprise is that of the Warrior Woman whom you had not identified at the encampment. In the Throne Room you recognise her haughtiness instantly. She is Cassandra, wanted by the priestesses of Illustra at Harith-si-the-Crow for the murder of their High Priestess, abetted by other dangerous worshippers of the insane god of chaos, Anarchil. You were attacked by three of them because you had slain their barbarian friend Olvar the Chaos Bringer in self-defence. Most clearly of all you remember that she is a breathtakingly swift swordswoman. Her magical Coldsword is now safe in your possession. Note that you have Cassandra's Sword on your Character Sheet. Turn to **71**.

202

The tunnels twist and turn. The Orcs can be heard following behind, all on foot now. They have to track by smell since they make so much noise, and you pull away from them. But Foxglove twists her ankle too badly to continue. If you have a Potion of Healing, Elixir of Health or Bag of Herbs, you may give it to her (turn to **222**), or you can wait for the Orcs to catch up with you and try to bluff it out (turn to **242**).

203

'Thaum was unwell following our last meeting with you. So unwell that we had, at great cost, to secure the services of a High Priest. It left Thaum a pauper.' Cassandra may be suggesting that he has been brought back from the dead, or perhaps that he was near mortally wounded. She goes on: 'There are many dark places in the Rift in which to hide. There is no telling whom you might meet, Avenger, in the everlasting darkness.' You ask Cassandra one more question. Will you ask where in the Rift Glaivas is being held (turn to **233**) or how many Dark Elves there are in the Rift (turn to **213**)?

204

The narrow way continues in a straight line for many hundreds of metres without opening out or offering any openings. Towards its end it climbs slightly, and when you are half way up the incline the floor tilts suddenly and pitches you all forwards on to your face in a small well-lit room hung with lush tapestries. When you stand and look around you receive something of a shock.

Turn to **244**.

205

Foxglove sleeps soundly, but you do not. Lack of sleep takes its toll when you begin to trudge on soon after dawn. Lose 2 Endurance and turn to **245**.

The swordsman is trying to charm you, using his magical sword Manmaster, but Foxglove's enchantment is too powerful and the magic of the sword has no effect. You become enraged that anyone should try to use magic to usurp the place of Foxglove in your favour. Foxglove asks you to teach them a lesson. If you have at least 2 points of Inner Force left, you are able to exert your will and self-control and overcome your desire to attack them. Lose 2 points of Inner Force and turn to **406**. If you wish to attack or do not have enough Inner Force left to go against Foxglove's wishes, turn to **238**.

The Dwarf-Trolls are armed with great axes that they swing with surprising control; each axe must weigh as much as a man. Owing to your quick thinking they have failed to steal the initiative, and you dodge the first sweeping blow. Will you back away and use the Iron Fist punch on any assailant (turn to **17**) or charge in with a Leaping Tiger kick (turn to **37**) or the Teeth of the Tiger throw (turn to **57**)?

Tyutchev grunts in pain and falls back as you go to deliver a killing blow. In the confusion you seem to come away with a pouch from his belt. Note that you have Tyutchev's Belt Pouch. You are about to try once more to finish him off when the tilting tunnelway that deposited you here in the hall tilts once more. You both leap back as four bodies fall into the room between you. They pick themselves up quickly, and you realise that they are acquainted with the three chaos-bringers with whom you have been battling. If you have already met a group of four men in the Rift, turn to **138**. If not, and if you have played Book 2: *ASSASSIN!* and defeated an Undead Warlord attacking a party of adventurers, turn to **144**. If you have played Book 2: *ASSASSIN!* and killed a magician who carried a gleaming Sun-star Ring, turn to **58**. If none of these applies, turn to **394**.

Too late you remember the teachings of Grandmaster Naijishi of the Island of Tranquil Dreams. 'When faced with a magician and a swordsman, always attack the spellcaster first.' As you are forcing the lithe Dark Elf soldier back, there is a magical explosion that robs you of your senses. You reel drunkenly and fall forwards on to the point of the sorceress's dagger, which finds your heart. Your end has come in the eternal darkness, far away from your home.

The tunnel curves gently for about half a kilometre before you see any sign of another soul. The Torch of Lumen shows a small ill-favoured Orc who had been walking towards you bowed down by the weight of a bundle of sticks he had been carrying. He stares at you for a few moments, then begins to back away, dropping the bundle. If you have a shuriken and wish to use it, turn to **230**. If not, turn to **250**.

Cassandra expects such tricks, having fought you before, and she has superb reactions. Your feet slide beneath her and you scissor your legs to topple her to the ground, but she leaps high and lands behind you. The tip of her sword gashes your arm as you whirl to face her and its unnatural cold bites into your bones. Lose 4 Endurance. If your Endurance is down to 3 or less, even 0 Endurance, turn to **191**. Otherwise you may strike again. Will you use the Cobra Strike punch (turn to **221**), the Forked Lightning kick (turn to **231**) or will you try to disarm her with a Whirlpool throw (turn to **241**)?

The Dark Elves shout a command in their lilting language, and when you are ten metres from the gallery they open fire. The volley of arrows comes thick and fast. If you have the skill of Arrow Cutting, turn to **312**. If not, turn to **332**.

'More than even you can hope to elude, Avenger,' responds the Warrior Woman glibly. Then: 'I will answer no more questions, but I will tell you this. When you reach the fourth tier, take the narrow way. The Way of Thrones has been baited as a trap for you, Avenger, a trap that even you cannot hope to survive.' Turn to **243**.

Thaum's weird gesticulations are a wonder to behold. Just as you set out to attack him there is an eruption of coruscating light so bright that it stuns you into immobility. You blink and realise that Cassandra and Tyutchev had expected it. They were not interested in the tapestry, merely anticipating the numbing flash that is the result of Thaum's sorcery. You reel backwards, blinded and helpless, wondering whether your fellow adventurers have suffered the same fate. Your question is answered when Cassandra's sword slices into your midriff. If you captured her sword outside the city, you lose 4 Endurance as her replacement sword is not magical. If she still has her Coldsword, the frost-rimed blade chills you to the marrow and burns in your wound. Lose 7 Endurance. If you still live, you are fortunate in that Thybault's flail cracks against her armour and she is forced to step back, allowing you time to recover. Turn to **414**.

'Glaivas is kept captive beyond the seventh tier in the area known as the Forbidden Sanctuary. The Black Widow's web reaches out from the hub there.' You ask Cassandra one more question. Will you ask how many Dark Elves there are in the Rift (turn to **295**) or where her friends Tyutchev and Thaum are to be found (turn to **315**)?

The four adventurers alter their appearance slightly, using magicians' skills, to the point where they could pass easily as creatures from the depths. Oddly enough your stealth while crossing the plaza appears to be wasted. Two Dark Elves moving silently from behind a guruka tree come face to face with you by accident, but they do not even seem to register your presence. By the time you near the stairway there is quite a press of people around you, but none of them seem about to raise the alarm or even speak. They stream down the twelve-metre-wide stairway which glows redly, like the stairway to hell, in the light of banks of fires on either side. Half way down are what look like perfect waxwork models of six Fire Giants, their dark hirsute bodies glowing in the rubescent firelight. They are as still as statues and no one even looks at them. Will you turn back (turn to **316**) or continue (turn to **336**)?

The narrow tunnel twists and turns ever deeper until it joins another near the second tier of the Rift. It is pitch black now, so you touch the Torch of Lumen and proceed carefully by its faint guiding light. Turn to **417**.

Your killing blow is effective enough. Cassandra sees the murderous look in your eye, but there is nothing she can do as her muscles tense in her efforts to stop the Worldworm closing its jaw. She shouts 'No', but crumples dead from a single blow. The sword falls out on to the ground below, and the Worldworm's jaws shut with an almighty crack, crushing you to death. You die far from home, deep in the eternal darkness.

Caught between the giant axes of the Dwarf-Trolls and the fiery breath and swords of the dragon-lizards and their riders, you decide to launch yourself over the edge into the bottomless dark and hope... You fall for what seems like an age before your body is broken on an outcrop of stone far from the light. Your end has come far from home in the darkness of the Rift.

220

The statues depict two beautiful Dark Elves. They are armed with slender adamantine scimitars, which are held up before their chests, and they face each other across the tunnel. Will you hurl yourself between the sword bearing statues (turn to **128**) or edge forwards carefully through the tunnel entrance (turn to **148**)?

221

Cassandra's gaze is unwavering as she searches your face for the slightest flicker that might betray the timing of your strike. You feint to strike high and then try to punch upwards underneath her guard. She has the reactions of a panther, and the tip of her sword whirs downwards to cut your arm.

CASSANDRA
Defence against Cobra Strike punch: 8
Endurance: 18
Damage: 1 Die +3

If you hit her and have reduced her to 12 Endurance or less, turn to **261**. Otherwise your Defence against her lightning riposte is 8. If you are reduced to 3 Endurance or less, even 0 Endurance, turn to **191**. Otherwise will you punch again (return to the top of this paragraph), use the Forked Lightning kick (turn to **231**), use the Dragon's Tail throw (turn to **211**), or attempt to disarm her using the Whirlpool throw (turn to **241**)?

Cross the item off your Character Sheet. Foxglove's well-being is restored. You run on and lose the Orcs, but you have also lost all sense of direction yourselves. Turn to **409**.

'Thaum was unwell following our last meeting with you. So unwell that we had, at great cost, to secure the services of a High Priest. It left Thaum a pauper.' Cassandra may be suggesting that he has been brought back from the dead, or perhaps that he was near mortally wounded. She goes on: 'There are many dark places in the Rift in which to hide. There is no telling whom you might meet, Avenger, in the everlasting darkness.' Then: 'I will answer no more questions, but I will tell you this. When you reach the fourth tier, take the narrow way. The Way of Thrones has been baited as a trap for you, Avenger, a trap that even you cannot hope to survive.' Turn to **243**.

You have fallen straight into the arms of a reception committee. Arranged in a semicircle about you are three people you recognise only too well. Directly opposite you is a tall wiry man whose frame is draped in a black cloak. The only hint of colour is his very curly hair, which is died bright corn yellow. He hefts a bastard sword almost negligently in one hand. On his right is a man in flowing grey robes covered with runes. He sports a large golden earring and has a look of devious intelligence and a smile of anticipation. On the other side is Cassandra, sword drawn, looking as haughty as ever, her bristling hair as dishevelled as her patchwork armour appears to be. The other two are her friends and your deadly enemies, Tyutchev, a thief and a blademaster, and Thaum, master of illusion and potent mage. They have done well to penetrate so deeply into the Bowels of Orb, for surely the Black Widow would kill them out of hand should she get the chance. Tyutchev likely found the secret stairway and, knowing that you could not descend the Fire Giants' Stair, they have lain in wait for you here. Turn to **264**.

225

You wake once during the night, to find Foxglove, still lying down, staring at you intently. As soon as she realises you are returning her gaze she turns over and pulls her sable fur around her head. You drift off to sleep again after a time and wake before her with the dawn. Turn to **245**.

226

Note that you have been charmed by Manmaster, the sword wielded by Vespers. The four adventurers are Eris the magician, Thybault and Taflwr, both priests, and Vespers, the swordsman. They are here in the Rift for a purpose, not merely to loot or to slay evil creatures. You have enemies in common. They are hunting three worshippers of the Chaos god Anarchil: Tyutchev, Thaum and Cassandra, the very people who seek your downfall. Thybault tells the story of how the evil three dared to venture into the great cathedral to Illustra and kill the powerful High Priestess before her own altar. Taflwr persuaded his friends to seek out and destroy the evil trio, whom they now suspect are somewhere on the fourth tier or below. If Foxglove is with you, turn to **386**. If not, they ask you to join them in their quest and to abandon your own for a while. Because you have been charmed you will find it difficult to do otherwise. If you choose to join them, turn to **306**. If you would like to refuse and you still have at least 2 Inner Force left, you may exert your will and wish them luck but refuse to join them. Turn to **326** but lose 2 points of Inner Force.

227

You flee just in time. The Dwarf-Trolls' chains snap taut just before they catch you and they begin to howl in annoyance, giving the alarm. You sprint back up the roadway towards the lip of the chasm, hoping to get out of sight before you are spotted by more intelligent foes. As you regain the lip you steal a quick look back. A figure stands beneath the first archway. A green and purple robe suggests it may be a Dark Elf, perhaps even a sister of Nullaq. She shields her eyes against the light and is staring up at you. Note that you have been spotted on the roadway. You dart out of sight and take the nearest twisting stairway that winds down out of sight between two spurs. Turn to **375**.

<h2 style="text-align:center">228</h2>

Foxglove has kept going well. She makes little sound, but her soft footfall lets you know that she is still right behind you. If you are both wearing the robes of Dark Elves, turn to **268**. If you are disguised as a shambler and Foxglove as your slave, turn to **288**. If you are relying on stealth alone to reach the lower levels, turn to **308**.

<h2 style="text-align:center">229</h2>

The sorceress falls under a hail of blows before she can marshal her thoughts and cast a spell. Just as you finish her there is a burning in your side. The soldier has picked up his sword and smitten you with it. Lose 5 Endurance. If you survive, you turn and parry his next attack before throwing him to the ground and disarming him. Though you are no expert with the blade, you manage to administer the coup de grace with it. Their clothing is not badly torn, so you gather their robes, belts and sandals plus two hoods that you find in a box. There is also a small jewelled pin, with a golden bullthrush for a head, inside an ivory box. Note that you have the Bullthrush Pin. If Foxglove is not with you, donning the green and red robe should be all the disguise you need, so you leave the other as well as the coffle chains you located earlier. Note your disguise and turn to **289**. If Foxglove is waiting, turn to **249**.

230

Make an Attack Roll against a Defence of 5. If you are successful, turn to **270**. If you miss, the Orc stoops to pick up the throwing star as he runs away. Cross off the shuriken from your Character Sheet and turn to **250**.

231

Cassandra looks into your eyes, watching for the flicker that will betray your strike the moment before it comes. You lash your foot out at her kneecap and then at the side of her head, but she recognises that the first attack is little more than a feint. Her sword shadows your foot and she moves with the speed of a panther, blocking you easily. Your leg is badly cut and stung by the cold of her sword. You lose 7 Endurance. If your Endurance is down to 3 or less, even 0 Endurance, turn to **191**. Will you respond with a Cobra Strike punch (turn to **221**), a Dragon's Tail throw (turn to **211**) or will you try to disarm her with a Whirlpool throw (turn to **241**)?

232

The Dark Elves give a series of commands in their lilting language and the Orcs and Ogres close in around you. 'What are you doing profaning the goddess's Sacred Vault?' says one. You can only guess which goddess this elfin sorceress is referring to, and you can only respond in the common tongue spoken by humans. Will you tell them that you live on the fourth tier, where legend has it there is or was a colony of evil humans living among other beings, and that you have come here to pray (turn to **70**) or surrender to them (turn to **90**)?

233

'Glaivas is kept captive beyond the seventh tier in the area known as the Forbidden Sanctuary. The Black Widow's web reaches out from the hub there.' Then: 'I will answer no more questions, but I will tell you this. When you reach the fourth tier, take the narrow way. The Way of Thrones has been baited as a trap for you, Avenger, a trap that even you cannot hope to survive.' Turn to **243**.

234

There is an eruption of coruscating light so bright that it almost stuns you into immobility, but by averting your gaze you remain in control. You blink and realise that Cassandra and Tyutchev had expected it. They were not interested in the tapestry, merely anticipating the numbing flash that is the result of Thaum's sorcery. They are darting to the attack already. Tyutchev's black cloak seems to deepen the darkness around him. Cassandra, as ever, moves with the grace and speed of a panther. Thaum is beginning another spell. Will you throw a shuriken at him, if you still have one (turn to **166**), or move aside so that you put Cassandra and Tyutchev between you and the master of illusion (turn to **178**)?

235

'More than even you can hope to elude, Avenger,' responds the Warrior Woman glibly. You ask Cassandra one more question. Will you ask her where in the Rift Glaivas is being held (turn to **275**) or where her friends Tyutchev and Thaum are to be found (turn to **315**)?

236

It takes more than a day to find an alternative to the Fire Giants' Stair. Meanwhile you eat food that you steal from the wicked denizens of the Rift, for the adventurers are out of supplies as well, and take what sleep you can. In the end, only by covertly watching the thieves of the twilit world, mainly Elves and Orcs who have their own thieves' cant – unlike any language you have heard – do you discover a secret doorway in a rock-face. It takes a little while to discover how the mechanism works, but at last you swing the rock aside and begin the descent. Turn to **276**.

237

You inch cautiously along the chasm wall on the inside of the roadway towards the bend. Peering around the corner confirms your fears. A great fortress of stone perched on a buttress of rock blocks your way. It is the gatecastle of the

first tier. The roadway runs right through the middle of the fortress, and there are guards in each of its towers as well as a motley group of creatures repairing the roadway before it. If you have the skill of Climbing and wish to use it, you may try to descend to the next tier down the sheer side of the chasm (turn to **79**). Otherwise you may try to slip through them all in the shadows (turn to **99**).

238

Your attack is ill-advised. The magician casts a spell that slows down the speed of your movement. As you struggle forward the movement of your opponents seems frightfully fast. Now the magical sword before you cleaves the air in a bewildering blur of motion. Slowed as you are, even you cannot long evade the wicked blade. You die deep in the eternal darkness, far from home.

239

Your blow, which has caught the Dwarf-Troll underneath the heart, has hit a vital nerve-centre and the beast falls, pole-axed, to the floor. You have killed the monster with a single blow. You are soon past the guard-post and continue on up the roadway hoping to get back to the lip of the Rift and then to descend into it again by a less busy route. The cold-blooded dragon-lizards begin to tire and you escape. Note on your character sheet that you have been spotted on the roadway and turn to **375**.

The torches set in brackets on the nearby walls seem to flare brightly of their own accord, throwing into vivid relief an etching on the floor which extends over most of the chamber in which you find yourself. The floor has been plated with metal on to which a huge bloated spider shape has been cut with acid. The spider has only four legs, one at each corner of its huge body, each of which points towards a tunnel exit. The tunnel by which you entered, to which the right back leg points, is suddenly blocked by a wall of flame, and the heat forces you forwards to the centre of the spider's body. A ghastly figure enters the chamber from the opposite tunnel. It is a Dark Elf in a robe of purple and green, but the usually beautiful jet-black face is horribly contorted. Eight splayed legs and a bloated spider's body project from below the chin, as if half a huge spider had been grafted on to her face. It is one of the sisters of Nullaq, dreaded magicians whose mothers have mated with one of the three Mother-Spiders in the deeper vaults of the Rift. She gestures you to leave the chamber by the tunnel indicated by the etching's front right leg. Foxglove falls to the floor with a sigh. She has fainted from horror. Will you pick up Foxglove's inert body and then leave by the indicated tunnel (turn to **180**)? If you choose to abandon her, will you leave by the indicated tunnel (turn to **160**), try to kill the sister of Nullaq and exit beyond her (turn to **200**) or try to leave by the other free entrance, guarded by two statues, behind you and to the left (turn to **168**)?

You step in close to draw her attack then dodge sideways and reach out to grab her wrist. Cassandra is trying to bury the tip of her sword in your vitals.

CASSANDRA
Defence against Whirlpool throw: 8
Endurance: 18
Damage: 1 Die +3

If you throw her successfully, you manage to wrest the sword from her grasp (turn to **261**). Otherwise your Defence against her terrible swift sword is only 6 as you have overcommitted yourself to this difficult manoeuvre and you may not block. If you are reduced to 3 Endurance or less, even 0 Endurance, turn to **191**. Otherwise you may strike again. Will you use the Dragon's Tail throw (turn to **211**), the Cobra Strike punch (turn to **221**) or the Forked Lightning kick (turn to **231**)?

242

You wait in tense anticipation for the arrival of the Orcs. To your annoyance Foxglove takes a healing potion from her cloak just as the Orcs arrive ready for battle. There is no time to flee. You will have to fight. Turn to **162**.

243

It would mean certain death for Glaivas, if he still lives, were you to detain Cassandra, so you tell her that she is free to leave and forbid her to enter the city again on pain of death. If you have Cassandra's Sword, you may decide for yourself whether she should be allowed to depart with it, and cross it from your Character Sheet if so. As she leaves, she says that you may yet meet her again. Now you must decide what to do about the plight of Glaivas. Any action you make should be taken quickly, lest Cassandra be spending her time brewing some terrible trap or ambush for you in the Rift. Turn to **393**.

244

You have fallen straight into the arms of a reception committee. Arranged in a semicircle about you are three people you recognise only too well. Directly opposite you is a tail wiry man whose frame is draped in a black cloak. The only hint of colour is his very curly hair, which is died bright corn yellow. He hefts a bastard sword almost negligently in one hand. On his right is a man in flowing grey robes covered with runes. He sports a large golden earring and has a look of devious intelligence and a smile of anticipation. On the other side is Cassandra, sword drawn, looking as haughty as

ever, her bristling hair as dishevelled as her patchwork armour appears to be. The other two are her friends and your deadly enemies, Tyutchev, a thief and a blademaster, and Thaum, master of illusion and potent mage. They have done well to penetrate so deeply into the Bowels of Orb, for surely the Black Widow would kill them out of hand should she get the chance. Tyutchev likely found the secret stairway and, knowing that you could not descend the Fire Giants' Stair, they have lain in wait for you here.

Turn to **284**.

245

On the next day Foxglove is sullen and will not speak to you. Tomorrow you will sight the last hills and forest before the Rift and you will have to set the horse free and continue on foot. When you camp at evening, however, she comes close to you, her eyes shining with tears, and says that she is too lonely and afraid to go on. 'Avenger, no one has shown me the smallest shred of kindness for longer than I can remember. I will go with you to the Rift, as I must, but if you do not embrace me now my heart will break and I shall lose my mind.' Will you comfort her as she desires (turn to **265**) or refuse her this kindness (turn to **285**)?

246

Thaum's fingers are making the strangest patterns in the air, and Cassandra and Tyutchev are looking at Foxglove. Will you look at Foxglove too (turn to **126**) or keep your eyes fixed on Thaum (turn to **146**)?

247

The Dwarf-Trolls are armed with great axes that they swing with surprising control; each axe must weigh as much as a man. You have to try to dodge or block the first sweeping blow. Your Defence is 7. If you are hit, you lose 6 Endurance. If you survive the first blow you have time to take the initiative. Will you back away and use the Iron Fist punch on any assailant (turn to **17**) or charge in with the Leaping Tiger kick (turn to **37**) or the Teeth of the Tiger throw (turn to **57**)?

248

If you are disguised as a Dark Elf, turn to **328**. If you are disguised as a shambler, turn to **348**. If you are relying on stealth and have no disguise, turn to **368**.

249

These clothes will serve better than any other you could procure. You choose the soldier's green and red garb for your own. Only female Dark Elves attain proficiency in the magical arts, so Foxglove will have to wear the blue robe of the sorceress. She is waiting for you still. She is probably quite lost already and must rely on you if she is ever to leave the Rift. She pulls back in alarm as she sees you striding towards her clad in the Dark Elf's robe and hood, but when she hears your voice she breathes a sigh of relief. Quickly she dons the blue robe and you are ready to plunge further into the dangers of the Rift. Note your disguise on your Character Sheet.

There is a choice of tunnels ahead of you. A small tunnel branches away deep into the rock, away from the direction of the cavern (turn to **409**), and a wider tunnel, which has rusty rails at one side of it, leads gently downwards and ahead (turn to **2**).

250

The Orc runs away uphill yelling 'Sunlander' for all he is worth. There is a cacophonous noise as of something rolling down the rails behind you and the cries of many Orcs. They are after you. You duck down a small side tunnel in an effort to lose them. You quickly become lost in a maze of tunnels, but eventually join another small tunnel leading downwards. Turn to **339**.

251

Later that day you order Cassandra and Foxglove to be brought into the Throne Room. Foxglove wears the same peacock gown that she wore when you first met her, when she petitioned to become a member of your Privy Council, but it is torn and travel-stained; the extravagant peacock tail train has been ripped off it long ago. She is still beautiful, but her beauty is that of the forlorn waif rather than the sophisticated courtesan. She seems frightened as much by the presence of Cassandra as by yourself. Fortunately, the Warrior Woman's magical Coldsword is now safe in your possession. Note that you have Cassandra's Sword on your Character Sheet. Turn to 71.

252

The echoing of your footsteps, no matter how stealthily you tread, returns from the faraway walls of the cavern. The feeling of being so far underground, surrounded by foes, is becoming overpoweringly unpleasant. The tension is unbearable; you feel trapped and vulnerable, and even begin to hear footsteps approaching that aren't there. When you are about half way across the vault, judging by the echoes, you realise that the footsteps are real and they are closing in on you from all sides. Suddenly there is a *whoosh* of flame, and a ring of fires bursts up ahead of you, then others to left and right. The vault is like a huge underground temple. Mock pillars that no longer quite reach the ceiling cast shadows at irregular intervals. The approaching footsteps are those of a party of Orcs led by two Dark Elves in blue cloaks. They have been walking towards the glow of the Torch of Lumen but now they can see you in the light of the fires. The chase is on. Ahead of you, thirty metres away, is a gallery leading to stairs, but it is guarded by a score of Orcs with crossbows. To the right, fifteen metres away, is another tunnel, but this is guarded by two Ogres wearing leather armour and wielding five-metre-long pikes like the men of Antiochis used in the golden age of the Inner Sea. To the left of you, about twelve metres away, are the Elves and Orcs. Will you run towards the Ogres (turn to 272) or the gallery (turn to 212) or stop where you are (turn to 292)?

253

Gwyneth and her troops had been powerless to help you, unable to scale the pinnacle in time, but now they reach the camp. Seeing you bloodied and in the hands of the enemy, they stop dead. Cassandra smiles and addresses you. 'I will say this only once, Avenger, so listen well. Your friend and trusted ally, Glaivas, the Ranger-Lord, has been taken prisoner by the Dark Elves in the Rift. Only one thing can save him. You must take the Sceptre that is your badge of rulership and surrender it to the Dark Elves inside the Rift. Then Glaivas will be released and you will both be allowed to go free. If you do not aid your friend in his hour of need, then you are no better than those who hold him prisoner in the everlasting darkness.'

She demands a safe departure for her war band now that she has delivered the message, and you grant it. The war band, with Foxglove in tow, marches back towards the Rift under the glowering eye of the Force-Lady. Note that Foxglove is Cassandra's prisoner. Once back at Irsmuncast you must come to a decision quickly. Turn to **393**.

254

Make a note of how many times you attack the thief. Tyutchev moves with the certainty and speed of a predator. You leap up and drive your foot at his neck, hoping to strike past his guard. If your attack succeeds and you have the skill of Yubi-Jutsu, you may add 2 to the damage, but you may not combine Nerve-Striking with Inner Force.

TYUTCHEV
Defence against Leaping Tiger kick: 9
Endurance: 20
Damage: 2 Dice + 2

If you hit him and have reduced him to 3 Endurance or less, turn to **208**. If you have not succeeded after three attacks, turn to **396**. Otherwise, your Defence against Tyutchev's riposte is 8. If you are still alive, you may use the Cobra Strike punch (turn to **181**), the Whirlpool throw (turn to **330**) or the Leaping Tiger kick again (return to the top of this paragraph).

255

'Thaum was unwell following our last meeting with you. So unwell that we had, at great cost, to secure the services of a High Priest. It left Thaum a pauper.' Cassandra may be suggesting that he has been brought back from the dead, or perhaps that he was near mortally wounded. She goes on: 'There are many dark places in the Rift in which to hide. There is no telling whom you might meet, Avenger, in the everlasting darkness.' You ask Cassandra one more question. Will you ask where in the Rift Glaivas is being held (turn to **275**) or how many Dark Elves there are in the Rift (turn to **295**)?

256

The Black Widow has set up a trap that even you cannot escape. As you walk past the thrones, a great slab of stone rumbles down into position at either end of the Way of Thrones, trapping you forever. You die next to statues of some of the most evil beings ever to walk the shadow world.

257

The chaos-bringers are aware of your tricks, and so when he sees a needle upon your lips, Tyutchev knows what is coming. He catches it on the flat of his blade but you have already changed plans. You dive into a roll, passing to Tyutchev's side and coming up in front of Thaum, who hardly has the time to react. There are scant moments to cripple the spellcaster before one or more of the swordfighters are upon you. Will you use the Tiger's Paw chop (turn to **22**), the Winged Horse kick (turn to **47**) or the Teeth of the Tiger throw (turn to **118**)?

258

You surrender to your assailants and Foxglove heaps scorn upon your head. She tells them that you are but her bodyguard, disguised to make journeying through the Bowels of Orb easier. She moves sensuously towards the swordsman, who seems to find her very charming. As she goes she tells them not to believe a word you say, describing you as a megalomaniac and a compulsive liar so sick that you believe you are Overlord of Irsmuncast nigh Edge. Will you protest that you really are Overlord (turn to **266**) or wait to see what happens (turn to **286**)?

259

Before you can rise from the ground the dragon-lizards and their riders arrive. You are bathed in flame and then savaged in one of the great monsters' jaws. Your end has come far from home in the darkness of the Rift.

260

The cavern swims before you and turns green as your brain switches to the picture seen by the emerald Orb which allows you to see the invisible. The sister of Nullaq has sidestepped two paces to the right, but you can see her clearly. Will you pretend that you cannot see her (turn to **300**) or continue your attack (turn to **158**)?

261

Your iron sleeves smash into the hilt of Cassandra's sword, which is knocked from her grasp and slithers away from her down the slope towards the river. She is a swordswoman, and without her blade she is no match for you, and she knows it. She turns to run, but you trip her and force her to surrender. To your surprise she puts up no further resistance as she allows you to tie her hands behind her back. She says proudly: 'Tyutchev, Thaum and I came close to killing you, Avenger, in the city of Harith-si-the-Crow. Why do you not now kill me? We are sworn enemies.' Will you change your mind and poison her with spiderfish venom (turn to **43**) or take her back to Irsmuncast (turn to **93**)?

262

Foxglove turns to you and says in the common tongue: 'How could you abandon me to these foul creatures?' Your mouth drops open as you are seized by abject shame and lost for words. The thought of what you have done robs you of your belief in yourself, for you have failed Foxglove, who is dearer to you than the rest of Orb put together. Lose all your remaining points of Inner Force. The chieftain of the Orcs recognises the common tongue, and he asks Foxglove who you are as she mounts the chariot beside him. He reaches out and paws her, but to your amazement Foxglove seems not to mind. Foxglove whispers in his ear. You should not be surprised to see that she can speak orcish, a legacy of her days organising the Order of the Yellow Lotus for the Usurper. Foxglove tells you to surrender to the Orcs. The nape of your neck bristles with fear, but you do as she says and are soon languishing in a grimy hole inside Sile's domain on the second tier. If you have the skill of Escapology, turn to **313**. If not, turn to **322**.

263

The fighting combined with your hunger has brought a throbbing pain to your head. The Dark Elf seems not to have carried anything of value on his person. Just in case the area is not as deserted as it appears, you hide his body in an alcove before proceeding. It is a long way between the third and fourth tiers and it is somewhat difficult to find the correct route. Evidently there are few connecting tunnels and stairways, so that the deeps are easily defensible against the attacks of Sunlanders in the unlikely event that an invasion of the twilit realms be attempted. You see no further sign of any trouble and skilfully evade detection until at last you find a way that leads down to the fourth tier. By this point, it is unlikely that disguise will do you further good; cross off any note about disguise from your Character Sheet. Turn to **56**.

264

The chaos-bringers are ready for you. Tyutchev says: 'Unlike your zealous Paladin friend, your path goes no further than this. At last, Avenger, the time has come for us to take our revenge, and you have brought us the Sceptre. Now I shall rule Irsmuncast.'

'You?' demands Cassandra, her striking features creased in anger.

'We shall all rule to the greater glory of Anarchil,' says Thaum in a calmer voice, 'and we shall destroy it utterly so that it passes beyond the memory of man.'

If Foxglove is with you, turn to **304**. If she is Cassandra's prisoner, turn to **18**. Otherwise, turn to **324**.

265

Foxglove comes into your arms and rests her head on your shoulder. An intoxicating aroma of exotic perfume, the scent of passion-flowers from the Island of the Goddess, wafts over you. You look into her eyes and marvel at her frail beauty. Before you can stop her she has stolen a kiss. Turn to **365**.

266

Your protestations are met with derisory laughter. Foxglove suggests that they tie you securely for your own good, lest you throw yourself against the walls of the cavern and injure yourself in a blind rage. They ask you to submit to this, which you do, feverishly thinking of a way to turn the tables on Foxglove. Suddenly a knife is at your throat and, unable to move, you feel your throat being slit. Foxglove has murdered you, and you will never turn the tables. Your people are alone without a saviour.

267

You instruct Foxglove to follow you quietly at an interval of twenty paces. She seems as frightened of you as of the denizens of the Rift and does exactly as you ask. You look back often to make sure that she is all right. Turn to **27**.

268

You wait for Foxglove to catch up as you stand in a dark cavern with fluted arches meeting at points in the ceiling. Hanging from each of the points is a skeleton, a grim reminder of the fate that befalls many here in the eternal darkness. There is a loud crack, and the cavern is lit up by vivid blue light. A lightning bolt from high up on the ceiling sizzles past you and strikes Foxglove, then rebounds off the

wall behind, striking the floor at your feet. Lose 2 Endurance. If you are still alive, you see that Foxglove is dead; the bolt of lightning has shattered her chest completely. Cross off any other notes about or effects involving Foxglove and note that she is dead. In the light of the bolt your acute senses picked up multiple man-shaped figures. Will you attack straight away (turn to **358**) or dive for cover through an archway (turn to **378**)?

269

The first needle embeds itself in the soldier's neck and he slumps to the floor just in front of you. The second, following swiftly, hits the sorceress in the eye just as she is casting a spell. She, too, falls. The spiderfish venom has done its work. You gather their robes, belts and sandals plus two hoods that you find in a box nearby. A smaller ivory box inside one of the hoods contains a small jewelled pin with a golden bullthrush for a head. Note that you have the Bullthrush Pin. If Foxglove is not with you, donning the green and red robe should be all the disguise you need, so you leave the other as well as the coffle chains you located earlier. Note your disguise and turn to **289**. If Foxglove is waiting, turn to **249**.

270

The shuriken fells the Orc and you pull it out of the warm body so that it can be used again. No one else disturbs your progress down the tunnel. Turn to **52**.

271

There are orcish sentries posted at intervals along the earthworks. Their night vision probably surpasses even your own, and it will be no easy task to slip past them. Will you use a stone to distract their attention (turn to **291**) or your flash powder (turn to **301**)?

272

The Dark Elves speak a command in their lilting language when you are six metres from the Ogres, but the Ogres seem too stupid to act quickly. The disguise has fooled them completely, and by the time they have swung their long pikes into action you have ducked between them and on down the exit tunnel. Note that you have been spotted in the Sacred Vault and turn to **372**.

273

Cassandra orders the Orcs to bind you hand and foot and leaves the camp so that she can examine the coveted emerald Orb alone. If you have the skill of Escapology, turn to **331**. If not, turn to **63**.

274

Thaum's weird gesticulations are a wonder to behold. Just as you set out to attack him there is an eruption of coruscating light so bright that it stuns you into immobility. You blink and realise that Cassandra and Tyutchev had expected it. They were not interested in the tapestry, merely anticipating the numbing flash that is the result of Thaum's sorcery. They are darting to the attack already but you can only guess at their actions from the noises you hear, for you are temporarily blinded and helpless. You reel backwards, but the tempered steel of Tyutchev's and Cassandra's meet in your vitals. You have been slain far from home, in the eternal darkness.

275

'Glaivas is kept captive beyond the seventh tier in the area known as the Forbidden Sanctuary. The Black Widow's web reaches out from the hub there.' Then: 'I will answer no more questions, but I will tell you this. When you reach the fourth tier, take the narrow way. The Way of Thrones has been baited as a trap for you, Avenger, a trap that even you cannot hope to survive.' Turn to **335**.

276

The twisting, turning tunnel soon branches into myriad other tunnels and caves. Mercifully this means you may avoid encountering the thieves of the twilit world. A sinister shadow moving on a nearby wall makes you start, but when you look again it is gone. You halt the group and listen, but all you can hear is the soft susurration of your own breathing. Turn to **4**.

277

You duck into the tunnel before anyone notices you and creep onwards, taking care always to descend towards the second tier. Turn to **417**.

278

Your Training of the Heart tells you that these four people, with the possible exception of the magician, who is a highly unreliable and capricious character but not wholly evil, are good and brave men. You can trust them, for they will not lie to you. It is clear, however, that they are unsure about you in turn. The swordsman waves his sword in your direction and speaks the words: 'Master of man and woman.' If you are enchanted by Foxglove, turn to **206**. If not, you find yourself beginning to like these four adventurers. Turn to **226**.

279

You abandon this frontal assault and let them chase you. When the time is right, you fling your grappling hook over your shoulder and up to the ceiling. Tyutchev, expecting an attack, recoils and allows your hook to catch on an arch. You immediately lunge to the side and pull yourself up with all your strength. You swing in a half-circle around the room, far out of reach of the chaos-bringers, before you disengage the hook and land beside Thaum, who hardly has the time to react. There are scant moments to cripple the spellcaster before one or more of the swordfighters are upon you. Will you use the Tiger's Paw chop (turn to **22**), the Winged Horse kick (turn to **47**) or the Teeth of the Tiger throw (turn to **118**)?

280

When Cassandra tore the emerald Orb from your face, she did more than inflict agony; she made you almost defenceless against invisible beings. Will you attack the point where you last saw the sister of Nullaq (turn to **340**), run out of the cavern down the tunnel she had indicated that is ahead of you and to your right (turn to **40**) or try to leave by the other free entrance, guarded by two statues, behind you and to the left (turn to **220**)?

281

After an hour's climbing, moving as the mountain lion patiently stalks the doe, you are at the top of the northern slope of scree, a very steep-sided wall of pebbles and slate chips. Not even a harvest-mouse could move silently over this scree. You pray to Kwon that you will avoid the notice of the orcish guards, whose night vision is so good. Courage buoys you up as you begin the difficult descent. Make a Fate Roll. If Fate smiles on you, turn to **351**. If Fate turns her back on you, turn to **361**.

282

Foxglove turns to you and says in the common tongue: 'We shall meet again, Avenger.' The chieftain of the Orcs recognises the common tongue and he asks Foxglove who you are as she mounts the chariot beside him. He reaches out and paws her, but to your amazement Foxglove seems not to mind. Foxglove whispers in his ear as you pretend not to have understood her words spoken in the common tongue. You should not be surprised that she can speak orcish, a legacy of her days organising the Order of the Yellow Lotus for the Usurper. Sile is far less interested in you than in she, however, and you are able to slink past them and away. You can hardly imagine where Foxglove's talents will carry her from here. Cross off any other notes about or effects involving Foxglove and note that she has become separated from you. Turn to **52**.

283

'I was brought, a prisoner of the Warrior Woman Cassandra, so that she would gain entry to the city and an audience with you, Overlord, all the more easily.'

You ask Foxglove to describe Cassandra.

'She is a cruel and heartless woman. I have never seen anyone handle a sword more skilfully than her, not even General Gwyneth. She has the speed of a cheetah.'

'What does she look like?' you enquire.

'She wears armour at all times, a curious patchwork of metal scales. Her hair is spiked like the spines of a hedgehog. Some would call her attractive... she is as cold as an icefish and has a sword to match.'

Foxglove's description has told you enough. It is the same Cassandra who is wanted by the priestesses of Illustra at Harith-si-the-Crow for the murder of their High Priestess, along with other dangerous worshippers of the insane god of chaos, Anarchil. You were attacked by three of them because you had slain their barbarian friend Olvar the Chaos Bringer in self-defence. Most clearly of all you remember that she is a breathtakingly swift swordswoman. Turn to **303**.

284

The chaos-bringers are ready for you but not for the four adventurers. The look of glee on their faces fades to one of uncertainty, while the four adventurers struggle hastily to their feet with looks of plain fear in their eyes, a fear that is quickly turned to hatred as Tyutchev speaks. 'I wonder that you dare to challenge us, or even that you survived this far. Unlike that zealous Paladin, you have not the power. Both Cassandra and I are more dangerous fighters than you, and you, fickle Eris, cannot rival Thaum's witchcraft.' Taflwr begins to chant a blessing in the name of Illustra. 'So that still rankles, does it?' asks Thaum, trying to break his concentration. Cassandra says: 'The High Priestess is dead. What is done cannot be undone. We have no vendetta against the followers of the Goddess of Life.'

'You who reverence Anarchil cannot keep an idea in your head for longer than a minute at a time,' says Thybault imperiously, 'but we do have a vendetta – against all who revere the insane god Anarchil.'

They are not even addressing you. The rivalry of these people must be deep-set. Tyutchev says to Eris: 'Come, Eris. You worship a Chaos god. Stand with us again. Cross over to the other side as you did once before. Otherwise your life is ruin, for you cannot stand against us.'

If Foxglove is also with you, turn to **344**. If she is Cassandra's prisoner, turn to **98**. Otherwise, turn to **364**.

285

You inform Foxglove that it is not fitting for an Overlord to embrace a commoner, but she is hurt. 'Then I shall kill myself. I cannot live despised by all.' She is suddenly wracked by sobs and seems to be completely distraught. It seems she really has nothing left to live for. Fear fills her life and you are leading her into the direst peril. Will you take her into your arms and comfort her (turn to **305**), tell her to go to sleep and save her strength for the descent into the Bowels of Orb (turn to **325**) or tell her you wish to search her before you allow her to touch you (turn to **345**)?

286

Foxglove suggests that you journey on together, deeper into the Rift. She places herself in the middle of the party, beguiling the swordsman called Vespers to protect her. You hear her speaking to the young swordsman, admiring his physique and generally flattering him. It is not long before they slip behind a pillar and are entwined in an embrace. Thybault, the priest of Avatar, becomes most dismayed when he realises what is happening, but when he remonstrates with Vespers, Foxglove tells him he is 'Naught but a cold-blooded priest who knows not the joys of living'. Foxglove is so beautiful and haughty that she makes him feel unsure of himself, and Vespers, pleased that Foxglove has chosen him, tells Thybault forcefully to be quiet. Note that Vespers is enchanted by Foxglove. Foxglove then turns from you to Vespers and says; 'If you care for me at all, young man, slay this troublesome imbecile.' She points out that you might shout out at an inopportune moment and cause their deaths. Vespers runs his thumb up and down the sharp blade of his magical sword and starts towards you. You must stop him. Will you attack (turn to **238**) or appeal to the priests to spare you (turn to **36**)?

287

Just as you turn to retrace your steps up the roadway there is the whir of a tomahawk flying through the air and a clatter as it strikes the side of the canyon nearby. You sprint away, stealing a look over your shoulder as you go – to see five Dwarf-Trolls, fat but powerful cross-breeds with pug-like faces, ranged across the road beneath the second archway. They are tethered there like dogs, chained to their guard-post; if you had walked on you would have been among them. They begin to howl, so you run on towards the lip of the Rift hoping to get out of sight before you are spotted by more intelligent foes. Foxglove manages to keep up well. She is tougher than she looks. Turn to **327**.

288

You are waiting for Foxglove to catch up, standing in a dark cavern with fluted arches meeting at points in the ceiling. Hanging from each of the points is a skeleton, a grim reminder of the fate that befalls many here in the eternal darkness. There is a loud crack and the cavern is lit up by vivid blue light. A lightning bolt from high up in the ceiling sizzles towards you, and you try to dive aside. It does not catch you with full force, but still you are thrown through the air and your nerves are horribly jarred. Lose 8 Endurance. If you are still alive, in the light of the bolt your acute senses picked up multiple man-shaped figures. Will you attack straight away (turn to **388**) or dive for cover through an archway (turn to **408**)?

289

There is a choice of tunnels ahead of you. A small tunnel branches away deep into the rock, away from the direction of the cavern (turn to **409**), and a wider tunnel, which has rusty rails at one side of it, leads gently downwards and ahead (turn to **353**).

290

Foxglove is taken away to a separate prison. You do not see her again, but word reaches you that she has been released before you decide the coast is clear and use your skills to break out of the prison. Cross off any other notes about or effects involving Foxglove and note that she has become separated from you. You are just in time to escape interrogation; the torture party arrives just as you are stealthily creeping away from the prison caves. Soon they are far behind. You find a tunnel that leads back towards the area of the Sacred Vault where you surrendered and then hasten onward.

Turn to **372**.

291

The sound of the stone crashing against the scree slope pulls one of the Orcs out of position on the earthwork. You seize your opportunity with the speed and control of the ninja, and silently steal towards the earthworks. If you have the skill of Picking Locks, Detecting and Disarming Traps, turn to **311**. If not, turn to **321**.

292

The Dark Elves see how you are dressed and seem fooled by the disguise. They say something in their lilting language and then lead the Orcs away from you once more. You are free to leave the chamber as the Orcs file out of the gallery. Turn to **372**.

293

Your ears pick up a subtle sound of movement and a Dark Elf swordsman in green and red lunges from behind a corner. You drop into a combat stance. 'Not this time!' he shouts, then cuts himself off and pulls up short before you. He holds his spare hand to his wounded side and looks haggard and desperate. You surmise that he is a survivor of the attack you passed earlier; perhaps he thought his assailants had followed him. Either way you must silence him immediately. Will you use the Iron Fist punch (turn to **175**), the Forked Lightning kick (turn to **185**) or the Dragon's Tail throw (turn to **195**)?

294

Your shuriken flashes across the hall and wounds Thaum in the shoulder – cross it off your Character Sheet, then roll one die and subtract the result from Thaum's Endurance of 12. He is no longer performing his incantations, but Tyutchev and Cassandra close on you simultaneously. Thybault and Vespers step bravely into the breach. They are skilled fighters. Thybault's flail whines as it whirls through the air and cracks as it smashes against Cassandra's armour. Her lightning riposte wounds the priest, but you are occupied with Tyutchev, who dares to attack both you and the swordsman Vespers together. Tyutchev parries the first swing from Vespers but this causes him to leave an opening and immediately you seize upon it. You dive into a roll, passing to Tyutchev's side and coming up in front of Thaum, who hardly has the time to react. There are scant moments to cripple the spellcaster before one or more of the swordfighters are upon you. Will you use the Tiger's Paw chop (turn to **22**), the Winged Horse kick (turn to **47**) or the Teeth of the Tiger throw (turn to **118**)?

295

'More than even you can hope to elude, Avenger,' responds the Warrior Woman glibly. Then: 'I will answer no more questions, but I will tell you this. When you reach the fourth tier, take the narrow way. The Way of Thrones has been baited as a trap for you, Avenger, a trap that even you cannot hope to survive.'

Turn to **335**.

296

The twisting, turning tunnel soon branches into myriad other tunnels and caves. Mercifully this means you may avoid encountering the thieves of the twilit world. A sinister shadow moving on a nearby wall makes you start, but when you look again it is gone. You listen, but all you can hear is the soft susurration of your own breathing.

If you have been spotted on the Fire Giants' Stair, turn to **356**. If not, turn to **416**.

297

Just as you are about to turn into one of the tunnels, a ghastly apparition surprises you. It is a Dark Elf in a robe of purple and green, but the usually beautiful jet-black face is horribly contorted. Eight splayed legs and a bloated spider's body project from below the chin, as if half a huge spider had been grafted on to the face. It is one of the sisters of Nullaq, dreaded magicians whose mothers have mated with one of the three Mother-Spiders in the deeper vaults of the Rift. She gestures and the air begins to shimmer before you like a

heat-haze. Then she launches a cloud of green dust that starts to descend upon you. As you glance down the tunnel, your avenue of escape, you glimpse a spider's web but nothing else of interest. Will you run down the tunnel (turn to **317**), advance into the shimmering haze (turn to **337**), stay where you are and hurl a shuriken if you have one (turn to **357**) or, if you do not have one, wait to see what happens (turn to **377**)?

298

You speak with them at length. Partway through, the swordsman waves his sword in your direction and speaks the words: 'Master of man and woman.' If you are enchanted by Foxglove, turn to **206**. If not, you find yourself beginning to like these four adventurers. Turn to **226**.

299

If Foxglove is with you, turn to **379**. If not, turn to **399**.

300

You stay absolutely still, appearing to look around questioningly but in reality waiting for her to step closer to you. When she does, you launch yourself in a great leap and lash out with a Leaping Tiger kick. If you do not have any Inner Force left, turn to **340**; otherwise subtract 1 point of Inner Force as you let out all your pent-up power with a cry. The sister of Nullaq is knocked down to lie sprawled at your feet but is fully conscious. She has become visible once more. If you wish to choose this moment to escape, will you run out of the cavern, down the tunnel she had indicated that is ahead of you and to your right (turn to **40**) or try to leave by the other free entrance, guarded by two statues, behind you and to the left (turn to **220**)? If you try to deal a killing blow, turn to **400**.

301

Cross the flash powder from your Character Sheet. As soon as the flash goes off there is uproar, and you realise from the meaningful sound of the orcish shouting that you have been spotted. They are not quick enough to catch you, however, and you return safely to Irsmuncast. Time is running out. Will you declare an amnesty for Foxglove and her companion (turn to **41**) or ride out with Gwyneth to take them by force (turn to **31**)?

302

Desperately you search for something small and slim to poke into your ear in an effort to dislodge the spider. In a flash you remember the jewelled pin. Whipping it out, you jab it gingerly into your ear and then pull it out again. On the sharp end is a small black and red spider, a miniature black widow. You wipe it off the pin on the side of the tunnel, squashing it. If you still have one of these tiny spiders inside your head, turn to **403**, otherwise read on.

You had unceremoniously dumped the inert figure of Foxglove on the ground when the spider fell on to your face. She seems to be coming round, and, in case anything worse is on its way, you hurry her to her feet. There are no sounds of pursuit as you continue searching for the paths that lead ever deeper into the ground, but the sensation of being watched grows until your hair prickles with apprehension. Turn to **52**.

303

'Why did Cassandra desire an audience with me?' you ask.

'She came to lure you into the Rift. The Dark Elves have captured Glaivas. They will put him to torture and kill him unless you give them the Sceptre which is the badge of your rulership. If you deliver the Sceptre to them they will let you and Glaivas go free. Cassandra hoped to kill you before you found Glaivas. She still burns for revenge.'

You ask of Doré, who had accompanied him, and she shakes her head. 'I do not know what became of the Paladin. I have told you all that I know. Now set me free, I beg you.'

'She is a traitress and should be put to the sword,' says Gwyneth.

Will you let Gwyneth have her way and order that Foxglove be executed for the part she is alleged to have played in the sack of your city (turn to **323**), let Foxglove go free on condition that she never enters the city again on pain of death (turn to **343**) or force her to accompany you to the Rift (turn to **363**)?

304

If you are enchanted by Foxglove, turn to **54**. If you are not, turn to **74**.

305

Foxglove comes into your arms and rests her head on your shoulder. An intoxicating aroma of exotic perfume, the scent of passion-flowers from the Island of the Goddess, wafts over you. You look into her eyes and marvel at her frail beauty. Before you can stop her she has stolen a kiss.

Turn to **365**.

306

The adventurers are heading towards the fourth tier. It is a long way between the third and fourth tiers and it takes some time for you to find a way down. Evidently there are few connecting tunnels and stairways so that the deeps are easily defensible against the attacks of Sunlanders in the unlikely event that an invasion of the twilit realms be attempted. You see no further sign of any trouble and skilfully evade detection until at last you find a way that leads down to the fourth tier. By this point, it is unlikely that disguise will do you further good; cross off any note about disguise from your Character Sheet.

If Foxglove is with you, turn to **136**. If not, turn to **156**.

307

As you near the second of the natural archways of stone your acute hearing picks up two sounds. One is the sound of rock on rock, the other the sound of metal on metal.

If you are interested in the sound of rock on rock, turn to **347**. If you are interested in the sound of metal on metal, turn to **367**.

308

You are crossing a dark cavern with fluted arches meeting at points in the ceiling. Hanging from each of the points is a skeleton, a grim reminder of the fate that befalls many here in the eternal darkness. A whispered warning carries to your sensitive ears: 'Assassin, challenge or slay?' Another whispers: 'Wait. What is a beauty like her doing here in the eternal dark?' There are at least two in the cavern who understand the common tongue. You know that they are about twelve metres ahead of you. Will you attack them (turn to **388**) or try to speak with them (turn to **338**)?

309

Tyutchev grunts in pain and falls back. You are about to finish him off when Thybault crashes into you, and somehow you come away with a pouch from Tyutchev's belt. Note that you have Tyutchev's Belt Pouch. Thybault had resumed battle but is losing against Cassandra, who has a killing light in her eyes. You steady him and move towards Cassandra. Eris and Taflwr are both recovered, but Thaum is about to cast another spell. Suddenly you notice the tapestry at one side of the room begin to ripple as if in a wind. Turn to **34**.

310

You are able to use your skills to break out of the prison and are just in time to escape interrogation; the torture party arrives just as you are stealthily creeping away from the prison caves. Soon they are far behind. You find a tunnel that leads back towards the area of the Sacred Vault where you surrendered and then hasten onward. Turn to **372**.

311

As you are about to leap the earthwork in one nimble bound, you notice that the earth feels strangely soft underfoot. Probing ahead carefully with a stick, you realise you are at the edge of a pit trap. Quickly you leap across it on to the earthwork itself and then lower yourself as quietly as a cat — and undetected — into the camp. Turn to **341**.

312

The Orcs let their bows fall in disbelief as you knock aside three arrows in quick succession and then catch one in each hand. You climb the steps to the gallery like a whirlwind and fell two of the Orcs who try to stop you. The Elves are still shouting orders as you disappear down the stairway at the far side of the gallery. Note that you have been spotted in the Sacred Vault and turn to **372**.

313

For five days you languish in the care of Lord Sile's Orcs, hoping and praying that Foxglove will at least come to visit you in honour of the heartfelt friendship you bear her. Then one day you overhear one of them saying in worried tones that Sile has gone mad and become infatuated with the woman Foxglove, who has ordered him to send you to the seventh tier, the Black Widow's lair. Almost too late you realise that you have been the victim of treacherous sorcery, and you see Foxglove in her true colours. Unfortunately you have had only the condensation which you could lick off the cave wall for sustenance these five days and have lost much of your strength. Lose 5 Endurance. If you are still alive, you regain the will to escape and use your skill to break out of the chains.

You slip out of Sile's domain and trace your way back to the point where you were captured before they have noticed you have gone. You can hardly imagine where Foxglove's talents will carry her from here. Cross off any other notes about or effects involving Foxglove and note that she has become separated from you.

Turn to **52**.

314

As you move, so does Cassandra – not towards you but towards Foxglove, who is cowering as far away as she can. Cassandra's sword is raised, ready to strike. If you want to protect Foxglove, turn to **94**. If, instead, you attack Tyutchev, who is running at you, turn to **152**.

'Thaum was unwell following our last meeting with you. So unwell that we had, at great cost, to secure the services of a High Priest. It left Thaum a pauper.' Cassandra may be suggesting that he has been brought back from the dead, or perhaps that he was near mortally wounded. She goes on: 'There are many dark places in the Rift in which to hide. There is no telling whom you might meet, Avenger, in the everlasting darkness.' Then: 'I will answer no more questions, but I will tell you this. When you reach the fourth tier, take the narrow way. The Way of Thrones has been baited as a trap for you, Avenger, a trap that even you cannot hope to survive.'

Turn to **335**.

As soon as you turn back, the creatures all around who had seemed oblivious to your presence begin to shout and try to grab hold of you. You fight your way to the top and it is only by the aid of your new allies that you do so without being wounded. Your martial skills and those of your companions are enough to deter your assailants once you reach the plaza again, and you lose yourself in the maze of tunnels. Note that you have been spotted on the Fire Giants' Stair.

Turn to **236**.

You run agilely down the tunnel. The sister of Nullaq does not give chase, but to your consternation she claps her hands and gives a repulsive laugh. If you wish to run back out into the cloud of green powder, turn to **377**. If you run on, turn to **397**.

The poison needle leaves your lips. The swordsman recoils into the arms of the priest in white. The priest plucks the dart from his friend's neck and speaks a short spell. The swordsman begins to sway unsteadily on his feet as the spiderfish venom takes hold, but then begins to recover as if he had suffered no worse than a wasp sting. He attacks, and their combined spells and weaponry are too potent to withstand. You die at their hands, deep in the eternal dark.

319

There is a choice of tunnels ahead of you. A small tunnel branches away deep into the rock, away from the direction of the cavern (turn to **339**), and a wider tunnel, which has rusty rails at one side of it, leads gently downwards and ahead (turn to **210**).

320

You run on. The flame behind you dies down for a moment and Foxglove enters the tunnel behind you, looking panic-stricken. Before you can calm her, the flame barrier ignites once more and a tiny spider drops from a recess in the roof of the tunnel onto your head. You slap at it but it runs through your hair into your ear, darting so quickly it cannot be stopped. If you have a Bullthrush Pin, turn to **8**. If not, turn to **28**.

321

All goes smoothly until you are about to leap the earthwork itself in one nimble bound, when the earth gives way beneath your feet and you fall into a pit trap full of spikes. You are not badly wounded, but a ring of spear-points above you heralds the arrival of the Orcs before you can escape. In the ruddy light of the fire you recognise a face you have seen before. She smiles haughtily and, unsheathing a sword rimed with frost and deathly cold, she beckons you out of the pit. She is Cassandra, wanted by the priestesses of Illustra at Harith-si-the-Crow for the murder of their High Priestess, along with other dangerous worshippers of the insane god of chaos, Anarchil. You were attacked by three of them because you had slain their barbarian friend Olvar the Chaos Bringer in self-defence. Most clearly of all you remember that she is a breathtakingly swift swordswoman.

Turn to **33**.

Once a week has passed Foxglove comes to visit you. Your heart leaps with joy. Perhaps she has not forgotten your friendship after all. But your hopes are cruelly dashed. She takes the Sceptre without so much as a word except to say that the idea of disguising yourself as a shambler and she as a slave was not a good one. 'I realised then that you were too stupid to take me all the way back to the Black Widow yourself.' The look of malicious triumph in her eyes speaks volumes. She will use the Sceptre to lead an army from the Rift against your city while you rot here powerless to stop her usurping your throne. You die in misery in the eternal darkness, far from home.

Gwyneth steps forwards and takes Foxglove's arm in a grip of iron. Foxglove screams in fear, but Gwyneth's face is set hard. She pulls the wailing woman out of your sight. The wails continue down the corridor and are then cut off abruptly. Gwyneth returns to the Throne Room alone. Note that Foxglove is dead.

You thank Gwyneth for performing the unpleasant duty of executing Foxglove. Gwyneth is used to living by the sword. 'It is part of my responsibility as general of the army of Irsmuncast,' she replies. When she has returned to her temple you ponder what to do about your poor friend Glaivas. Turn to **393**.

Thaum's fingers are making the strangest patterns in the air, and Cassandra and Tyutchev are looking away to the side of the hall. Will you look at the tapestry too (turn to **234**) or keep your eyes fixed on Thaum (turn to **274**)?

There is a sudden flash of anger in Foxglove's eyes, then she does as you bid. Bedding down on the far side of the camp fire, she turns her back on you and swathes herself in her sable cloak. Will you stay awake all night to make sure

Foxglove does not escape or try to kill herself (turn to **385**) or sleep soundly so that you are refreshed for the descent into darkness tomorrow (turn to **405**)?

326

They wish you luck as well as you leave them. Soon they are nothing but a memory, left far behind in this labyrinthine maze of tunnels and caverns far from the sunlight. It is a long way between the third and fourth tiers and it takes some time for you to find a way down. Evidently there are few connecting tunnels and stairways so that the deeps are easily defensible against the attacks of Sunlanders in the unlikely event that an invasion of the twilit realms be attempted. You see no further sign of any trouble and skilfully evade detection for hour after hour. By this point, it is unlikely that disguise will do you further good; cross off any note about disguise from your Character Sheet. Turn to **56**.

327

You regain the top of the canyon before pursuers appear on the roadway below you, and take the nearest of the smaller twisting stairways; it winds down out of sight between two spurs. Turn to **415**.

328

You are crossing a dark cavern with fluted arches meeting at points in the ceiling. Hanging from each of the points is a skeleton, a grim reminder of the fate that befalls many here in the eternal darkness. There is a loud crack, and the cavern is lit up by vivid blue light. A lightning bolt from high up in the ceiling sizzles towards you, and you try to dive aside. It does not catch you with full force, but still you are thrown through the air and your nerves are horribly jarred. Lose 8 Endurance. If you are still alive, in the light of the bolt your acute senses picked up multiple man-shaped figures. Will you attack straight away (turn to **358**) or dive for cover through an archway (turn to **378**)?

329

You push away from the rock-face and drop away from the clutches of the Firedrake. You fall for what seems an age before your body is broken on an outcrop of stone far from the light. Your end has come far from home in the eternal darkness of the Rift.

330

Make a note of how many times you attack the thief. Tyutchev's bastard sword parts the air with a menacing shrill sound and you duck to let it fall beyond your shoulder. Your arm darts out parallel to the blade and you wrap it around his wrist, as you intend to twist into him and throw him over your hip. However, Tyutchev's skill with the sword is as the dancers with their feet, and he is already using his momentum and yours to drive the blade back and into your upper leg. Any greater force and your leg would have been sheared clean off. As it is, you lose 6 Endurance.

If you still live, and if this was your third attack, turn to **396**. Otherwise, you can use the Cobra Strike punch (turn to **181**) or the Leaping Tiger kick (turn to **254**).

331

When the Orcs bind you they are as intent on hurting you as binding you tight, imagining that if you try to escape they will have the pleasure of beating you senseless. You tense your limbs and, when you are ready, relax. The bonds fall loose and you squirm free before they realise what is happening. As you make your escape, running faster than any Orc can, you hear Cassandra calling for the cat o' nine tails. The poor Orcs who bound you will regret their lack of vigilance. You are back at Irsmuncast in a few hours, but you have tipped your hand, and you decide that further violence would serve no useful purpose. You offer amnesty to Foxglove and your enemy Cassandra. Turn to **85**.

332

Three of the arrows find their mark though fortunately each leaves only a shallow wound. Lose 6 Endurance. If you are still alive, you pluck them out while you are running. With one leap you gain the gallery and fell two of the Orcs who try to stop you. The Elves are still shouting orders as you disappear down the stairway at the far side of the gallery. Note that you have been spotted in the Sacred Vault and turn to **372**.

333

Foxglove looks nervously at Cassandra, who glowers at her, before replying. 'The Dark Elves took Glaivas two days before we set out from the Rift. They want the Sceptre. I do not know what became of the Paladin.' She hesitates, and you prompt her to go on. She breaks into a flood of words: 'They will kill you, Avenger. It is a terrible place! The gods themselves could not survive in the Bowels. The air is tainted with poison and death and there are monsters that lurk there in the depths larger than cities... ' She is breathing rapidly, her breast rising and falling with emotion. 'The Dark Elves are cruel and depraved beyond imagining. Don't send me back there with that woman, Overlord, I beg you.' Cassandra sneers at her in disgust. Turn to **123**.

334

Make a note of how many times you attack the thief. Tyutchev grins evilly as he moves in to the attack. His enormous bastard sword swirls through the air faster than you might have believed possible and you can only hope to strike even faster. If your attack succeeds and you have the skill of Yubi-Jutsu, you may add 2 to the damage, but you may not combine Nerve-Striking with Inner Force.

TYUTCHEV
Defence against Cobra Strike punch: 7
Endurance: 20
Damage: 2 Dice + 2

If you hit him and have reduced him to 3 Endurance or less, turn to **309**. If you have not succeeded after three attacks, turn to **360**. Otherwise, Tyutchev easily deflects another attack from Vespers and then his blade arcs in a backwards swing up underneath your outstretched arm. Your Defence is 9. If you are still alive, you may use the Leaping Tiger kick (turn to **402**), the Whirlpool throw (turn to **418**) or the Cobra Strike punch again (return to the top of this paragraph).

335

It would mean certain death for Glaivas, if he still lives, were you to detain Cassandra, so you tell her that she is free to leave and forbid her to enter the city again on pain of death. If you have Cassandra's Sword, you may decide for yourself whether she should be allowed to depart with it, and cross it from your Character Sheet if so. As she leaves she says: 'We may yet meet again, Avenger, or are you too craven to take up the quest?' Now you must decide what to do about the plight of your poor friend Glaivas. Any action you make should be taken quickly, lest Cassandra be spending her time brewing some terrible trap or ambush for you in the Rift. Turn to **105**.

336

As you pass beneath the Fire Giants the other creatures either hurry on or lag behind. When the immobile Giants come suddenly to life, you are surrounded by them. Their unseeing eyes, like dark stones, seem to gaze above your head, but when the clubs start crashing down one after the other they are all perfectly synchronised and on target. Their sixth sense has told them you are an interloper and they need no eyes to see, for they have the inner eye. They are not the largest of the giant race but they are among the strongest. Their clubs strike great boulders from the rock stair and you are soon a thin smear on the rock. You have died far from home in the eternal darkness.

337

You leap into the shimmering air ready to close and do battle, but find yourself choking and gasping. Feeling as though you had been without water in a desert for hours on end, you begin to crave your own blood to drink. To resist slashing your own wrist to bring forth a river of blood calls for a major effort of will. If you have the skill of ShinRen, you lose only 1 point of Inner Force from your current score. If you lack this skill, you lose 2 points of Inner Force. If you do not have enough Inner Force remaining, you suspect Kwon is lending you strength, for still you resist the temptation and burst out of the shimmering haze, whereupon the illusion of thirst leaves you. Before you can attack, the sister of Nullaq turns into a black crow. She leaps off the lip of the ledge outside the store-houses and is soon lost in the darkness of the chasm below. You decide to go on a few metres before taking to one of the tunnels. Turn to **9**.

338

Foxglove stays back as you tell them urgently that you are none other than the Overlord of Irsmuncast nigh Edge and of your quest to rescue Glaivas, your Ranger friend. As soon as you speak their attitude to you changes and you have the opportunity to study them closely. If you have played Book 2: *ASSASSIN!* and defeated an Undead Warlord attacking a party of adventurers, turn to **78**. Otherwise read on.

The swordsman wears a grey surcoat with an unfurled scroll picked out in white thread across his chest. Your studies in the library at Irsmuncast tell you this is the insignia of a reverencer of the god Gauss. The man in the white robe is a priest. He sports the cross of Avatar on his chest. The third man is in green and is also a priest, though he wears chainmail, a worshipper of Illustra, Goddess of Life. The fourth, the magician, is a worshipper of a Chaos god. The five-spoked wheel insignia shows the Limitless Possibilities that may lead to good acts, however, rather than those that may lead to evil. He had been hovering in the air and now descends gently to the ground. If you have played Book 2: *ASSASSIN!* and killed a magician who carried a gleaming Sun-star Ring, turn to **352**. Otherwise read on.

They are good people, unless they are in disguise. If you have the skill of ShinRen, turn to **278**. If not, they demand to know more so that they may judge your intentions. Will you trust them (turn to **298**) or use Poison Needles if you have that skill (turn to **318**)?

339

The narrow tunnel ends abruptly in a steep stone stairway shelving deeply down. Since Glaivas is almost certainly many tiers below, you decide to take the stairs. After a long climb you come to the edge of a great cavern. It is far too big for the Torch of Lumen to cast light on its far side. Alert to the slightest sound, you set off across the immense vault. Turn to **172**.

340

Your blow finds only empty air. There is a terrible burning in your side – you have been stabbed. A patch of blood spreads quickly across your clothes. Lose 6 Endurance. If you are still alive, you decide that you cannot hope to defeat this enemy. Will you run out of the cavern, down the tunnel she had indicated that is ahead of you and to your right (turn to **40**), or try to leave by the other free entrance, guarded by two statues, behind you and to the left (turn to **220**)?

341

You discern two figures sleeping a little way away from the malodorous Orcs. One has merely unlaced her armour. The hilt of her sword glints in the moonlight near her outflung hand. The other must be Foxglove – her dark curling tresses show up on the light soil and she is wrapped in a threadbare travelling cloak. You can try to knock one of them out with a minute dose of spiderfish venom and then attempt to carry her off. Will you try to capture Foxglove (turn to **371**) or the Warrior Woman (turn to **381**)?

342

The spider burrows deeper and deeper inside your ear. Desperately you shake your head and cuff yourself, hoping to dislodge it, but to no avail. Soon you can feel it fidgeting somewhere under your brain. It is a daughter of Nullaq. If you now have two of these daughters of Nullaq spiders inside your head, turn to **68**. If not, note that you are carrying a daughter of Nullaq and turn to **403**.

343

Foxglove leaves the Throne Room in indecent haste and you order her an escort of shieldmaidens so that she may leave the city without being stoned. Note that Foxglove is exiled.

Gwyneth seems barely able to suppress her annoyance and says: 'Overlord, have you taken leave of your mind? She will not rest until her intriguing has brought your downfall and delivered our city of Irsmuncast into the hands of the Riftspawn.' Will you order Gwyneth to be quiet and strip her of command of the army (turn to **413**) or say that you value her judgement but that you cannot order even a former leader of the Yellow Lotus, the Usurper's secret informers, to be summarily executed without full proof (turn to **5**)?

344

If you have been enchanted by Foxglove, turn to **384**. If not, and if Vespers has been enchanted by Foxglove, turn to **404**. If Taflwr has been enchanted by Foxglove, turn to **14**. If none of these applies, read on.

Foxglove, whose powers in such a situation are limited, sinks to the floor and makes herself small, hoping that when the spells start to fly she will be overlooked.

Turn to **246**.

345

'That will not be necessary, Avenger,' says Foxglove. 'This is what you would have been looking for.' She slips a stiletto knife out of a pocket in the lining of her sable cloak, unsheathes it and holds the blade up before you. The point glistens with green venom. She sheathes the knife and throws it to the ground beside you, saying: 'My only defence against the Riftspawn.' Then she holds out her arms to embrace you. Reasonably certain that she is not going to try to kill you, you stretch your arms out warily.

Turn to **265**.

346

They heed your warning and tell Foxglove not to speak unless spoken to. Thybault says: 'By your actions we shall judge you in the name of Avatar the One.' Foxglove appears frightened of him and keeps quiet, apart from beseeching them to protect her from danger. They do seem interested in travelling with you, not so much for her sake as to recruit your assistance in their own quest. Will you continue with them (turn to **306**) or say: 'May Fate smile on you' and go your own way, taking Foxglove with you (turn to **326**)? If you have been charmed by the sword of Vespers you will find it difficult to part ways. You may only do so by expending 2 points of Inner Force to exert your will.

347

You look up to see a small shard of rock which has broken away from the wall of the canyon above tumbling down the rock-face to land on the roadway at your feet. At the same instant there is the whir of a tomahawk flying through the air at you. If you have the skill of Arrow Cutting, turn to **367**. Otherwise read on. You whirl around, but it is too late. Foxglove slumps to the ground, the tomahawk embedded in her back. You duck as a boulder nearly smashes your head. The sound of metal on metal that you heard was the faintest scraping of the chains that tether your assailants to the archway. Five Dwarf-Trolls, fat but powerful cross-breeds with pug-like faces, are ranged across the road beneath the second archway. They are tethered there like dogs, chained to their guard-post, but they lurch forwards with giant ungainly strides to assail you. Will you stand over Foxglove and give battle to protect her (turn to **387**) or flee (turn to **407**)?

348

You are crossing a dark cavern with fluted arches meeting at points in the ceiling. Hanging from each of the points is a skeleton, a grim reminder of the fate that befalls many here in the eternal darkness. A muffled exclamation carries to your sensitive ears: 'What on Orb is that?' There are at least two in the cavern who understand the common tongue. You know that they are about twelve metres ahead of you. Will you attack them (turn to **358**) or try to speak with them (turn to **16**)?

349

The grappling hook and rope become tangled around the enormous Firedrake, which shies away from you at the last moment. It takes the rope and hook with it, however – note the loss on your Character Sheet. You are forced to let go or be dragged from your precarious position to fall in the bottomless pit of the Bowels of Orb. The Demiveult flies down into the blackness to find its roost and disentangle itself. You are left stranded without your rope. Your only option is to climb up again, for if you continue downwards and come to a place where rope is needed you will be too exhausted to turn back. Turn to **389**.

350

The torches set in brackets on the nearby walls seem to flare brightly of their own accord, throwing into vivid relief an etching on the floor which extends over most of the chamber in which you find yourself. The floor has been plated with metal on to which a huge bloated spider shape has been cut with acid. The spider has only four legs, one at each corner of its huge body, each of which points towards a tunnel exit. The tunnel by which you entered, to which the right back leg points, is suddenly blocked by a wall of flame, and the heat forces you forwards to the centre of the spider's body. A ghastly figure enters the chamber from the opposite tunnel. It is a Dark Elf in a robe of purple and green, but the usually beautiful jet-black face is horribly contorted. Eight splayed legs and a bloated spider's body project from below the chin, as if half a huge spider had been grafted on to her face. It is one of the sisters of Nullaq, dreaded magicians whose mothers have mated with one of the three Mother-Spiders in the deeper vaults of the Rift. She gestures you to leave the chamber by the tunnel indicated by the etching's front right leg. Will you do so (turn to **40**), try to kill the sister of Nullaq (turn to **20**) or try to leave by the other free entrance, guarded by two statues, behind you and to the left (turn to **220**)?

351
Miraculously you achieve the almost impossible. It takes another hour to descend the fifteen-metre scree slope, and your muscles are aching from the effort of exerting such iron control over your limbs. At last you are within the enemy encampment undetected. Turn to **341**.

352
This is the man you killed while ferrying the Scrolls of Kettsuin back to the Temple of the Rock, whose Sun-star Ring you took but that you could not use. You do not know what means brought his recovery, but he shows no sign of remembering the event, or at least of recognising you as that ninja. You consider his comrades, who should not know you at all. If you have the skill of ShinRen, turn to **278**. If not, will you trust them (turn to **298**) or use Poison Needles if you have that skill (turn to **318**)?

353
If Foxglove is with you, turn to **359**. If not, turn to **2**.

354
As you move, so does Cassandra – not towards you but towards Foxglove, who is cowering as far away as she can. Cassandra's sword is raised ready to strike. Foxglove cries out to Vespers to protect her, and he gallantly bars Cassandra's way. Tyutchev is running towards you, so you prepare to give battle. He swings his bastard sword at your head as though the weapon weighed nothing. The blade rings off of your iron sleeves and in an instant is coming at you from the opposite direction. You parry again but find it difficult to counter attack, for the cloak he wears makes his position uncertain. You realise you cannot maintain this forever, and soon Thaum will turn the tables with his spellcraft unless you can disable him.

You must get beyond the swordfighters to reach Thaum. Will you use Acrobatics (turn to **161**), Poison Needles (turn to **257**), Climbing, if you still have your grappling hook and rope (turn to **279**) or, if you cannot or choose not to use these skills, force your way through Cassandra and Tyutchev (turn to **76**)?

355

You lash out a crippling blow with your fist, seeking to despatch these Orcs before they can overwhelm you. You may choose only one to attack at a time.

	CHARIOTEER ORC	FIRST ORC	SECOND ORC
Defence against Punch:	6	5	5
Endurance:	10	8	7
Damage:	1 Die + 1	1 Die	1 Die

If you are able to defeat two, turn to **132**. Your Defence against their attacks is 8. Each has an individual attack and you may only block one of them. If you survive, you may use the Iron Fist punch again (return to the top of this paragraph) or the Winged Horse kick (turn to **373**).

356

Passing a small alcove, you catch sight of a strange samovar encrusted with large sapphires. It is about sixty centimetres tall and made of solid gold. Will you examine it (turn to **44**) or pass on by (turn to **24**)?

357

Make an Attack Roll. The sister of Nullaq, who has been surprised by the speed of your throwing star, tries to duck but her Defence is only 6. If you hit, turn to **19**. If you miss, turn to **59**.

358

With all the speed and power of a tiger, you move to the attack. A man in white stands closest but gives back before you. He is armed with a flail that has golden chains. You are faster than he and soon close to do battle, but as you do so you become aware of his allies. A swordsman who wields his sword in his left hand and carries a scroll in his right moves from behind an archway to your left. A third figure in armour and green garments stands further back. Above you, hovering in the air near the ceiling, is a man in a dark robe with a golden five-spoked wheel emblazoned on his chest – a magician. He speaks a spell. A shining silver javelin appears in his hand and is launched towards you. As it flies, it grows a serpent's head. Your Defence is 6. You must rely on your agility and may not try to block. If you are hit, turn to **6**. If not, turn to **65**.

359

The tunnel curves gently for perhaps half a kilometre before you see any sign of another soul. The Torch of Lumen shows a small ill-favoured Orc who had been walking towards you bowed down by the weight of a bundle of sticks he had been carrying. He is mesmerised by Foxglove's beauty, and looks from you to her several times before dropping the bundle and loping off uphill. You hurry, hoping to come to a dividing of the ways so that you can leave this tunnel.

You are urging Foxglove on when there is a cacophonous noise behind. A wagon is rolling down the rails towards you, still as yet out of sight, but you can hear the groans of a straining band of Orcs, harsh cries and the occasional crack of a whip. Will you turn and run, abandoning all pretence at disguise (turn to **42**), or go on as you are (turn to **62**)?

360

You are still struggling with Tyutchev when Thybault crashes into you. He had resumed battle but is losing against Cassandra, who has a killing light in her eyes. You steady him and move towards Cassandra. Eris and Taflwr are both recovered, but Thaum is about to cast another spell. Tyutchev turns to face the new threat from his one-time friend, Eris the Magician. Suddenly you notice the tapestry at one side of the room begin to ripple as if in a wind. Turn to **34**.

361

One unlucky step starts a small torrent of pebbles rolling that turns into an avalanche. Your arrival in the enemy camp could not be more spectacular as you plummet towards the river almost buried in scree. Before you can dig yourself out, a ring of spear-points above you heralds the arrival of the Orcs. In the ruddy light of the watch fire you recognise a face you have seen before. She smiles haughtily and, unsheathing a sword rimed with frost and deathly cold, she beckons you forward. She is Cassandra, wanted by the priestesses of Illustra at Harith-si-the-Crow for the murder of their High Priestess, along with other dangerous worshippers of the insane god of chaos, Anarchil. You were attacked by three of them because you had slain their barbarian friend Olvar the Chaos Bringer in self-defence. Most clearly of all you remember that she is a breathtakingly swift swordswoman. Turn to **33**.

362

Lord Sile is surprisingly fast, and he doesn't fall for your feint Instead he catches your foot on your second kick and puts you flat on your back. Lose 5 Endurance. The Orcs cheer and he comes forwards again, pretending to stamp on your groin but instead driving his fist into your face. All you can do is try to roll aside. Your Defence against his blow is only 4. If he hits you, lose 4 more Endurance. If you are still alive you flip backwards in a somersault on to your hands and then on to your feet once more. The Orcs stop laughing and Lord Sile's face betrays surprise but no fear. Will you use the Tiger's Paw chop (turn to **382**), Kwon's Flail, if you remember being taught this kick in a previous adventure (turn to **12**) or the Teeth of the Tiger throw (turn to **32**)?

363
You have Gwyneth take Foxglove to the donjon, the small windowless tower at the north-east corner of the Palace, which she does none too gently. Next you ponder the difficult situation that confronts you.

Turn to **105**.

364
Thaum's fingers are making the strangest patterns in the air, and Cassandra and Tyutchev are looking away to the side of the hall. Will you look at the tapestry too (turn to **194**) or keep your eyes fixed on Thaum (turn to **214**)?

365
If you have the skill of ShinRen, turn to **15**. Otherwise turn to **35**.

366
Foxglove suggests that you journey on together, deeper into the Rift. She places herself in the middle of the party, beseeching the priest called Taflwr to protect her. You hear her speaking to the young priest. She is telling him a tale of such woe that the poor man is almost moved to tears. She makes him feel that he has a mission to convert her to the faith of Illustra, Goddess of Life. It is not long before they slip behind a pillar and are entwined in an embrace. Thybault, the priest of Avatar, becomes most dismayed when he realises what is happening, but when he remonstrates with Taflwr, Foxglove tells him he is 'Naught but a cold-blooded priest who knows not the joys of living'. Foxglove is so beautiful and haughty she makes him feel unsure of himself, and Taflwr, pleased that Foxglove has chosen him, tells Thybault politely but firmly to be quiet. Note that Taflwr is enchanted by Foxglove. Thybault still

mistrusts her, but he falls into line behind you all and you continue together.

Turn to **306**.

367

With a speed that defies belief, you sweep your arm across. There is the ring of metal on metal as your iron sleeves collide with the blade of a tomahawk and send it spinning harmlessly away into the depths of the chasm. You have saved Foxglove's life. You drop to your haunches as a small boulder flies at your head. It shatters against the rock-face behind you. The sound of metal on metal that you heard before was the faintest scraping of the chains that tether your assailants to the archway. Five Dwarf-Trolls, fat but powerful cross-breeds with pug-like faces, are ranged across the road beneath the second archway. They are tethered there like dogs, chained to their guard-post, but they lurch forwards with giant ungainly strides to assail you. You yell at Foxglove to flee, and lead her back towards the lip of the chasm. The Dwarf-Trolls begin to howl the alarm, and you hurry on hoping to gain the top of the canyon before more intelligent foes catch sight of you. Foxglove keeps up well; she is tougher than she looks. Turn to **327**.

368

You are crossing a dark cavern with fluted arches meeting at points in the ceiling. Hanging from each of the points is a skeleton, a grim reminder of the fate that befalls many here in the eternal darkness. A whispered warning carries to your sensitive ears: 'Assassin, challenge or slay?' There are at least two in the cavern who understand the common tongue. You know that they are about twelve metres ahead of you. Will you attack them (turn to **358**) or try to speak with them (turn to **16**)?

369

You struggle upwards just as the Firedrake tries to grab you with its outstretched talons. It fails to pluck you from the rock-face, but your back is badly scored. Lose 4 Endurance.

Your rope is cut, too – note the loss of your grappling hook and rope on your Character Sheet. The Firedrake loses height then wheels away towards other prey. You have had a lucky escape. You are left stranded without rope. Your only option is to climb up again, for if you continue downwards and come to a place where rope is needed you will be too exhausted to turn back. Turn to **389**.

370

There are no sounds of pursuit as you continue searching for the paths that lead ever deeper into the ground, but the sensation of being watched grows until your hair prickles with apprehension. Turn to **52**.

371

Foxglove stirs uneasily and shivers a little as you approach, but you prick her neck and the venom does its work. She convulses once, then lies rigid and still. You wait until clouds cover the starry sky and then retreat across the earthwork. Foxglove is slim and weighs little – indeed, she seems almost undernourished. By dawn you are two kilometres from the encampment, and a farmer is honoured to take you both back to Irsmuncast in his ox-cart.

Turn to **391**.

372

For several hours you follow the circuitous twistings of the tunnels that lead down, towards the third tier somewhere below. Your nerves are strained taut like hot wires lancing into your brain. The constant sense of peril is not lessened by the hours spent with no danger in sight; rather, dread only increases, as it becomes easy to imagine you walk a path designed to carry you to your doom. If the walls themselves were shifting on you, you could never tell.

You strike upon larger halls, perhaps the very lowest inhabited parts of the second tier. Approaching footsteps startle you out of your thoughts. If Foxglove is with you, turn to **140**. If she is not, read on. If you were spotted crossing the Sacred Vault on the second tier, turn to **350**. Otherwise, turn to **370**. You only count as having been spotted if you were instructed to make a note on your Character Sheet.

373
The Orcs charge forward with hardly any regard for their own well-being. You may choose only one to attack at a time.

	CHARIOTEER ORC	FIRST ORC	SECOND ORC
Defence against Punch:	6	5	5
Endurance:	10	8	7
Damage:	1 Die + 1	1 Die	1 Die

If you are able to defeat two, turn to **132**. Your Defence against their attacks is 8. Each has an individual attack and you may only block one of them. If you survive, you may use the Iron Fist punch (turn to **355**) or the Winged Horse kick again (return to the top of this paragraph).

374
As you move, so does Cassandra – not towards you but towards Foxglove, who is cowering as far away as she can. Cassandra's sword is raised, ready to strike. Foxglove cries out to Taflwr to protect her, but he can do no more than look blindly in her direction and groan. If you want to protect Foxglove, turn to **94**. If, instead, you attack Tyutchev, who is running at you, turn to **152**.

375
The nearest stairway is crumbling and unused, and the steps are half-eroded in places, but you make your way steadily down into the gloom. After half an hour's climb, in which time you have seen no living creature, you come to a gallery of caves served by many tunnels and paths cut into the side of the canyon wall. You have reached the first tier and are already in a twilit world. You touch the Torch of Lumen and it casts a gentle glow about you. You will need its light from here on. Turn to **27**.

376

As soon as you turn back, the creatures all around who had seemed oblivious to your presence begin to shout and try to grab hold of you. You fight your way to the top, but not without being wounded. Lose 4 Endurance. If you still live, your martial skills are enough to deter your assailants once you reach the plaza once more, and you lose yourself in the maze of tunnels. Note that you have been spotted on the Fire Giants' Stair. Turn to **176**.

377

The powder settles all around you and begins to burn into your flesh like acid. Lose 4 Endurance. If you are still alive, you look up again to see the sister of Nullaq turn into a black crow. She leaps off the lip of the ledge outside the storehouses and is soon lost in the darkness of the chasm below. You decide to go on a few metres before taking to one of the tunnels. Turn to **9**.

378

You reach cover just in time. Another bolt of lightning just misses you, ricocheting from wall to wall with thunderous cracks. Will you try to speak with your assailants (turn to **16**) or race to the attack (turn to **358**)?

379

Foxglove has followed patiently and quietly every step of the way, at a safe distance. In the dim light of the Torch of Lumen it is hard to read her expression when she nears, but she shows no signs of leaving you or giving you away, nor has she asked for any more proofs of your devotion. Finding a disguise for yourself alone will not be very useful if you cannot disguise Foxglove as well. You tell her to wait quietly and then set out to find the two disguises that you need. Turn to **419**.

380

Foxglove seems to have recovered from her faint. She beseeches you, for reasons beyond understanding, to leave the cavern by the tunnel indicated by the sister of Nullaq. Her voice is so soft, calm and reassuring that you find yourself taking her advice. Cross off any other notes about or effects involving Foxglove and note that she has become separated from you.

Turn to **40**.

381

The Warrior Woman seems to be sleeping deeply. You prick her neck and the poison does its work. She convulses once and goes rigid, but her eyes are still open and she is struggling to whisper something. You lean closer and hear: 'Do not kill me. If I die, so does one loved by Overlord Avenger of Irsmuncast.'

'What is this?' you hiss.

'Cure me of the poison that burns me so and I will tell you.'

Will you give her the antidote (turn to **3**) or carry her off out of the camp (turn to **13**)?

382

Lord Sile is faster than you expected. He strikes first, pretending to try to trip you before letting loose a great roundhouse punch. Your Defence is 7. If he hits you, lose 4 Endurance. If you are still alive, you counter-attack with a Tiger's Paw chop.

LORD SILE THE ORC CHIEFTAIN
Defence against Tiger's Paw chop: 7
Endurance: 18
Damage: 1 Die + 2

If you win, turn to **72**. One of the Orcs hurls a stone at you. You knock it aside, but this has given Lord Sile time to lash out at you with his foot. If you survive, will you use the Forked Lightning kick (turn to **362**), the Tiger's Paw chop (return to the top of this paragraph), Kwon's Flail, if you remember being taught this kick in a previous adventure (turn to **12**) or the Teeth of the Tiger throw (turn to **32**)?

383

You hear footsteps and a Dark Elf swordsman in green and red runs out from behind a corner. You drop into a combat stance. He is shouting something in the lilting language of his kind, but he cuts himself off and pulls up short before you. He holds his spare hand to his wounded side and looks haggard and desperate. You surmise that he is a survivor of the attack you passed earlier; perhaps you fooled him into thinking help had arrived. Either way you must silence him immediately. Will you use the Iron Fist punch (turn to **175**), the Forked Lightning kick (turn to **185**) or the Dragon's Tail throw (turn to **195**)?

384

Note that if you are given the choice of protecting Foxglove from attack, you must always choose to do so. Thaum's fingers are making the strangest patterns in the air, and Cassandra and Tyutchev are looking at Foxglove. Foxglove calls you to her side to be her protector. You turn and run to do her bidding just as there is an eruption of coruscating light so bright it almost stuns you into immobility. You blink and realise that Cassandra and Tyutchev had expected it. They were not interested in Foxglove, merely anticipating the numbing flash that is the result of Thaum's sorcery. They are darting to the attack already. Tyutchev's black cloak seems to deepen the darkness around him. Cassandra, as ever, moves with the grace and speed of a panther. You are lucky you were not looking at Thaum, for you would surely have been stunned by the flash had you not averted your eyes. The four adventurers have not all been so lucky. Vespers reacted quickly enough to shield his eyes and Thybault too has not been stunned, but Eris the Magician and Taflwr are reeling back in a state of shock. Will you use a shuriken against Thaum, who is beginning another spell, if you have one (turn to **294**) or move aside so that you put Cassandra and Tyutchev between you and the master of illusion (turn to **314**)?

385

Foxglove sleeps soundly, but you do not. Lack of sleep takes its toll. Lose 2 Endurance then turn to **115**.

386

They ask who Foxglove is, and you are about to tell them when Foxglove butts in. 'I was brought up to the worship of Nemesis, Supreme Principle of Evil. I became a servant of the evil Usurper of Irsmuncast, then when Avenger became Overlord I served faithfully but to no avail. I was cast out of the city and blamed for its sack. I wish to renounce the faith of Nemesis.' She looks beseechingly at the kind face of Taflwr, Priest of Illustra. You can already see Taflwr softening towards her. Will you warn them against trusting Foxglove (turn to **346**) or let matters take their own course (turn to **366**)? If you are enchanted by Foxglove, one look of reproach is enough to silence you and you can only let matters take their course and turn to **366**.

387

You step over Foxglove's slumped body, your own body tensed for battle like a tiger ready to spring. The Dwarf-Trolls are armed with great axes that they swing with surprising control; each axe must weigh as much as a man. You have to try to dodge or block the first sweeping blow. Your Defence is 7. If you are hit, you lose 6 Endurance. If you survive the first blow you have time to take the initiative. Will you back away and use the Iron Fist punch on any assailant (turn to **117**) or charge in with the Leaping Tiger kick (turn to **137**) or the Teeth of the Tiger throw (turn to **57**)?

388

Foxglove backs quickly out of danger as, with all the speed and power of a tiger, you move to the attack. A man in white stands closest but gives back before you. He is armed with a flail which has golden chains. You are faster than he and soon close to do battle, but as you do so you become aware of his allies. A swordsman who wields his sword left-handed and carries a scroll in his right moves from behind an archway to your left. A third figure in armour and green garments stands further back. Above you, hovering in the air near the ceiling, is a man in a dark robe with a golden five-spoked wheel emblazoned on his chest, a magician. He speaks a spell. A shining silver javelin appears in his hand and is launched towards you. As it flies, it grows a serpent's head. Your Defence is 6. You must rely on your agility and may not try to block. If you are hit, turn to **6**. If not, turn to **65**.

The effort is almost too much for you as you climb back towards the roadway above. At last you clamber back on to the roadway. Unfortunately you have come up in front of the gatecastle. A cry rings out from one of the towers. You have been spotted. You have no choice but to continue your retreat the way you came as four Dark Elves, riding flightless dragon-lizards, charge out of the gatehouse. An arrow from one of the towers finds its mark but causes only a flesh wound. Lose 4 Endurance from the exhaustion of the climb and from the wound. If you are still alive, you round a corner in the road and near the guard-point manned by Dwarf-Trolls once again. If you are skilled in Acrobatics, turn to **119**. If you do not have this skill, you must fight your way through (turn to **139**).

This passage too begins to descend and then becomes a twisting stairway. Food soon becomes a concern as you have run out of supplies. Your knowledge of plant lore will do you no good if nothing edible grows. Soon you must find new sustenance.

For several hours you follow the tortuous twistings of the stairway down to the third tier. Your nerves are at their breaking point; tension and hunger make your head throb. You have been listening for sounds of pursuit for so long that you can no longer tell whether the distantly muffled commands and the dull echo of a great gong that seems to sound every time you set off down another turn in the staircase is real or imagined. Turn to **401**.

Turn to **401**.

391

Later that day Gwyneth arrives at the Palace with the news that the Orcs and their leader have retreated back towards the Rift. Gwyneth stays with you in the Throne Room to interview Foxglove. When Foxglove enters the Throne Room gracefully you realise she is wearing the same peacock gown that she wore when you first met her and she petitioned to become a member of your Privy Council, but it is torn and travel-stained, the extravagant peacock tail ripped off it long ago. She is still beautiful, but her fragile beauty is that of the forlorn waif rather than the sophisticated courtesan you remember.

Even as Foxglove curtsies, Gwyneth fires an accusation at her. 'So, traitress, you have returned to Irsmuncast, the city that you betrayed to the dross that issued forth from the Bowels of Orb? Why did you open the city gates to the enemy?'

'It was not I who opened the gates. Please believe me.'

'Opened the gates to the enemy and when the enemy were beaten you fled to their land beneath the earth.'

'I fled because I would not be believed. Once the rumour that I was a traitress began, there was nothing I could do.'

You decide to ask Foxglove why she has been brought back to the city. Turn to **283**.

Foxglove has not run after you. She has given up all chance of escape and is surrendering. You will have to continue your mission to save Glaivas without her. Cross off any other notes about or effects involving Foxglove and note that she has become separated from you. If you have the skill of Acrobatics and wish to use it, turn to **30**. Otherwise turn to **50**.

To take the Sceptre into the Bowels of Orb is to expose it and yourself to the gravest danger. Yet you remember how Glaivas has already indebted you to him many times over. If it were not for the warning of Glaivas that fateful day on the Island of Tranquil Dreams, your god Kwon would have been incarcerated in Inferno. Today you would probably not now be Overlord of the city, as he risked his life for you in battle against the Legion of the Sword of Doom. Your course is clear: you will risk all to save your friend.

You cannot ask another to share with you the dangers of the Rift. In any case, stealth is your greatest asset, so you must journey alone. You take the Sceptre and swathe it in black cloth, then hide it inside your ninja costume. Leaving Gwyneth orders to publish the news that you are journeying to meet two saviours of the city, you prepare to set off to that darkest pit of evil, the Bowels of Orb. One other artefact you take from the royal armoury. This is the Torch of Lumen, an ebony rod topped by a cone of alabaster. When the alabaster is touched it gives off a constant light that will be invaluable in the eternal darkness of the Rift. It was enchanted by your father's most powerful sorcerer and looks to all but its bearer as an ordinary brazier.

You receive healing if necessary before you depart. Restore your Endurance to 20 if you were wounded. Turn to **125**.

The four are all men. They seem to be a party of adventurers. One in a grey surcoat with an unfurled scroll picked out in white upon it is a swordsman. A priest wears the white robe and red cross of Avatar, the Supreme Principle of Good, another priest the green robe and white cross of Avatar's consort, Illustra, Goddess of Life. The fourth is a magician sporting the five-spoked wheel on his robe, which indicates he worships Béatan the Free.

Their faces as they take in who they have stumbled across are quite comical. They line up for battle. There is fear in their faces, but this quickly turns to anger when Tyutchev speaks. 'I wonder that you dare to challenge us. You have not the power. Both Cassandra and I are more dangerous fighters than you, and you, fickle Eris, cannot rival Thaum's witchcraft.'

The priest in green begins to chant a blessing in the name of Illustra. 'So that still rankles, does it?' asks Thaum, trying to break his concentration.

Cassandra says: 'The High Priestess is dead. What is done cannot be undone. We have no vendetta against the followers of the Goddess of Life.'

'You who reverence Anarchil cannot keep an idea in your head for longer than a minute at a time,' says the other priest imperiously. 'But we do seek vengeance, against all who worship the insane god Anarchil.'

They are not even addressing you. You realise the rivalry of these people runs deep. Suddenly you notice the tapestry at one side of the room begin to ripple as if in a wind. Turn to **34**.

395

The road winds gradually downhill, criss-crossing the canyon face in kilometre-wide zigzags. Every now and then it burrows into the rock, cutting through a spur that makes a natural archway of stone above the road. At the first there are signs of a deserted guard-post. If you wish to turn back and take the narrow path, turn to **67**. If not, turn to **87**.

396

You are still struggling with Tyutchev when the tilting tunnelway that deposited you here in the hall tilts once more. You both leap back as four bodies fall into the room between you. They pick themselves up quickly, and you realise that they are acquainted with the three chaos-bringers with whom you have been battling. If you have already met a group of four men in the Rift, turn to **138**. If not, and if you have played Book 2: *ASSASSIN!* and defeated an Undead Warlord attacking a party of adventurers, turn to **144**. If you have played Book 2: *ASSASSIN!* and killed a magician who carried a gleaming Sun-star Ring, turn to **58**. If none of these applies, turn to **394**.

397

As you run on there is the lightest tremor in the web that spans the tunnel. You duck, but a tiny spider drops into your ninja hood. You unfurl the black cloth to shake it off, only to feel the spider run across your face and up your nostril. You sneeze automatically, but to no avail. You can feel the little spider fidgeting somewhere under your brain. Note that you are carrying a daughter of Nullaq. For now, there seems nothing else to do but continue walking on.

Turn to **417**.

398

If you captured Cassandra's sword before setting out to the Rift, turn to **53**. If not, turn to **420**.

399

It should not be too hard to find yourself a disguise here on the second tier. You wait and listen for some time before deciding on the direction to take, hoping it is one that will lead you to creatures of some sort but not into the arms of too many at once.

Turn to **419**.

400

You are too quick for the sister of Nullaq this time. Your blow breaks her neck and robs her of life. Quickly searching her body, you find a Potion of Healing. You may use this at any time, except when in battle, to restore up to 10 lost

Endurance points. Not wasting another moment, you leave by the tunnel through which she entered the cavern, not wishing to be discovered here. Turn to **370**.

401

At last you reach the huge halls of the third tier. The atmosphere is filled with smoke that burns the lungs until you become used to it. At least the braziers burning everywhere mean you can conceal the Torch of Lumen for the time being. Together with the smoke you become aware of a constant hum in the background. This puzzles you for some time until you realise it is the everyday noise of the denizens of the third tier going about a multiplicity of mundane tasks, the sound of their voices and the scuffing of their shoes blended with many thousands of other noises into a monotonous low drone. If Foxglove is with you, turn to **228**. If not, turn to **248**.

402

Make a note of how many times you attack the thief. Tyutchev moves with the certainty and speed of a predator. You leap up and drive your foot at his neck, hoping to beat past his guard while Vespers distracts him with his own blows. If your attack succeeds and you have the skill of Yubi-Jutsu, you may add 2 to the damage, but you may not combine Nerve-Striking with Inner Force.

TYUTCHEV
Defence against Leaping Tiger kick: 8
Endurance: 20
Damage: 2 Dice + 2

If you hit him and have reduced him to 3 Endurance or less, turn to **309**. If you have not succeeded after three attacks, turn to **360**. Otherwise, your Defence against Tyutchev's riposte is 9. If you are still alive, you may use the Cobra Strike punch (turn to **334**), the Whirlpool throw (turn to **418**) or the Leaping Tiger kick again (return to the top of this paragraph).

403

The spider moves occasionally, as if to remind you to live in fear, but nothing awful happens yet. You look to Foxglove. You had unceremoniously dumped her inert figure on the ground when the spider fell on to your face. She seems to be coming round, and, in case anything worse is on its way, you hurry her to her feet. There are no sounds of pursuit as you continue searching for the paths that lead ever deeper into the ground, but the sensation of being watched grows until your hair prickles with apprehension.

Turn to **52**.

404

Thaum's fingers are making the strangest patterns in the air, and Cassandra and Tyutchev are looking at Foxglove. Foxglove calls Vespers to her side to be her protector. You see him turn and run to do her bidding just as there is an eruption of coruscating light so bright it almost stuns you into immobility. You blink and realise that Cassandra and Tyutchev had expected it. They were not interested in Foxglove, merely anticipating the numbing flash that is the result of Thaum's sorcery. They are darting to the attack already. Tyutchev's black cloak seems to deepen the darkness around him. Cassandra, as ever, moves with the grace and speed of a panther. You are lucky you were not looking at Thaum, for you would surely have been stunned by the flash had you not averted your eyes. The four adventurers have not all been so lucky. Vespers has been saved by the distraction and Thybault too has not been stunned, but Eris the Magician and Taflwr are reeling back in a state of shock. Will you use a shuriken against Thaum, who is beginning another spell, if you have one (turn to **294**) or move aside so that you put Cassandra and Tyutchev between you and the master of illusion (turn to **354**)?

405

Make a Fate Roll. If Fate smiles on you, turn to **135**. If Fate turns her back on you, turn to **155**.

Foxglove seems to dismiss the failed idea and replace it just as quickly with another. She suggests that you journey on together, deeper into the Rift. She places herself in the middle of the party, beguiling the swordsman called Vespers to protect her. You hear her speaking to the young swordsman, admiring his physique and generally flattering him. It is not long before they slip behind a pillar and are entwined in an embrace. Thybault, the priest of Avatar, becomes most dismayed when he realises what is happening, but when he remonstrates with Vespers, Foxglove tells him he is 'Naught but a cold-blooded priest who knows not the joys of living'. Foxglove is so beautiful and haughty she makes him feel unsure of himself, and Vespers, pleased that Foxglove has chosen him, tells Thybault forcefully to be quiet. Note that Vespers is enchanted by Foxglove. Foxglove is ready now to continue.

As you go, you have a chance to listen to the group. The four adventurers are here in the Rift for a purpose, not merely to loot or to slay evil creatures. You have enemies in common. They are hunting three worshippers of the Chaos god Anarchil: Tyutchev, Thaum and Cassandra, the very people who seek your downfall. Thybault tells the story of how the evil three dared to venture into the great cathedral to Illustra and kill the powerful High Priestess before her own altar. Taflwr, the other adventuring priest, persuaded his friends to seek out and destroy the evil trio, whom they now suspect are somewhere on the fourth tier or below. Turn to **306**.

You flee just in time. The Dwarf-Trolls' chains snap taut just before they catch you and they begin to howl in annoyance, giving the alarm. One of them crushes Foxglove's head underfoot. Cross off any other notes about or effects involving Foxglove and note that she is dead. You sprint back up the roadway towards the lip of the chasm, hoping to get out of sight before you are spotted by more intelligent foes. As you regain the lip you steal a quick look back. A figure stands beneath the first archway. A green and purple robe suggests it may be a Dark Elf, perhaps even a sister of Nullaq. She shields her eyes against the light and is staring up at you. Note that you have been spotted on the roadway. You dart out of sight and take the nearest twisting stairway that winds down out of sight between two spurs. Turn to **375**.

408

You reach cover just in time. Another bolt of lightning just misses you, ricocheting from wall to wall with thunderous cracks. Will you try to speak with your assailants (turn to **338**) or race to the attack (turn to **388**)?

409

The narrow tunnel ends abruptly in a steep stone stairway shelving deeply down. Since Glaivas is almost certainly many tiers below, you decide to take the stairs. After a long climb you come to the edge of a great cavern. It is far too big for the Torch of Lumen to cast light on its far side. Alert to the slightest sound, you set off across the immense vault. Turn to **252**.

410

The path you tread now is the most desolate yet. After an indeterminate amount of time you realise you must be bypassing the entire third tier. At last you come into more open spaces and seek a way down towards the fourth tier. Food is scarce and you have run out of supplies. Your knowledge of plant lore will do you no good if nothing edible grows. Soon you must find new sustenance. If you are dressed in Dark Elf clothing, turn to **383**. If dressed any other way, turn to **293**.

411

The end of the hallway slides back to reveal a bowl-shaped cavern running with fire. It is the lair of the Worldworm, which fables tell has its head in the Rift, here, and a body that stretches all the way around Orb, through the roots of the mountains, and a tail that reaches to the very centre of

Orb. In the middle of the bowl is what looks like a gigantic statue of a snake's head, its mouth open, showing great curving fangs. Tyutchev does not hesitate, for there is no other way out of the cavern. He leaps into the statue's open mouth and is lost to view. You sprint towards the statue as the Krathak's stinking breath bathes you and its footfalls shake the earth. Soon everyone has jumped into the statue's mouth. Cassandra is the last, just ahead of you. As she leaps there is a cracking noise and the statue turns to grey-green scaly flesh. The Worldworm is coming to life. As quick as thought, Cassandra thrusts her blade into the roof of the Worldworm's mouth to prevent its closing upon her. In the next instant you have leaped up beside her. The Krathak is not far behind. Will you attempt a killing blow against Cassandra (turn to **218**) or run into the belly of the Worldworm (turn to **398**)?

Will you attempt a killing blow against Cassandra (turn to **218**) or run into the belly of the Worldworm (turn to **398**)?

412

Foxglove leaves you for dead, but you sink into a trance and let your body overcome the poison. When you are well enough to continue, Foxglove is nowhere to be seen. You must continue your mission to the Rift alone. Note that Foxglove has become separated from you. Turn to **165**.

413

'I will no longer tolerate your veiled opposition to my wishes, General Gwyneth' you say quietly. 'You are relieved of command of the army. Kindly return to your temple.'

Gwyneth says just as quietly: 'You cannot rule without me, Avenger. The army is loyal to me.' And she draws her sword and advances, shield ready to divert a shuriken. Will you apologise to her and reinstate her as General of Irsmuncast (turn to **25**) or give battle (turn to **45**)?

414

When you recover you quickly notice that the priest Taflwr and Eris the Magician have been stunned. Thaum is beginning another spell. Thybault stands between you and Cassandra, his flail thrumming as it whirls through the air. Will you use a shuriken against Thaum, who is beginning another spell, if you have one (turn to **294**) or move left so that you put Thybault and Cassandra between you and the master of illusion (turn to **106**)?

415

The nearest stairway is crumbling and unused, and the steps are half-eroded in places, but you make your way steadily down into the gloom. After half an hour's climb, in which time you have seen no living creature, you come to a gallery of caves served by many tunnels and paths cut into the side of the canyon wall. You have reached the first tier and are already in a twilit world. You touch the Torch of Lumen and it casts a gentle glow about you. You will need its light from here on. Turn to **267**.

416

At last the stairs stop in a great dimly lit hallway of dressed stone. A magnificent and sinister sight greets you. Away to the left is a huge archway, and beyond it a succession of carven thrones with statues of the former rulers of this part of the Bowels of Orb. In the shadows you can glimpse apparitions, the sight of which would freeze the blood of ordinary folk. To the right is a tall but very narrow tunnel, so

narrow that it will admit only one abreast. Will you walk down the Way of Thrones (turn to **256**) or the narrow way (turn to **184**)?

417

Many tunnels converge on a cavern where you make out a fresco that chills your blood. It shows a great web with a black widow spider, identifiable by the scarlet hour-glass shape on its back, testing all the lines from the web with her legs. At each extremity is a smaller version of her, crawling over some poor unfortunate – Orc, Dark Elf or human; even an Old One is shown trying in vain to free itself from a silken web. Another fresco shows a Paladin in full armour but without helm. He is being assailed by the small spiders, which seem to be creeping into his ears, nose and, as he screams, his mouth. Turn to **9**.

418

Make a note of how many times you attack the thief. Tyutchev's bastard sword parts the air with a menacing shrill sound and you duck to let it fall beyond your shoulder. Your arm darts out parallel to the blade and you wrap it around his wrist, as you intend to twist into him and throw him over your hip. However, Tyutchev's skill with the sword is as the dancers with their feet, and he is already using his momentum and yours to drive the blade back and into your upper leg. Any greater force and your leg would have been sheared clean off. As it is, you lose 6 Endurance.

If you still live, and if this was your third attack, turn to **360**. Otherwise, you stagger behind Vespers, whose blade clashes against that of Tyutchev once again as you ready your next move. You may use the Cobra Strike punch (turn to **334**) or the Leaping Tiger kick (turn to **402**).

419

For an hour you scour the tunnels and caverns of the second tier. They are as lively as the streets of a market town, but the darkness discourages conversation. The people of the second tier, low in the hierarchy of power, are too busy conserving enough energy to keep alive to indulge in frivolity. Several times you are almost spotted, but at length you come to a cavern with a stone façade built across its front, like a house. You can clearly hear the sinisterly musical voices of two Dark Elves inside. They must have clothes that you could use as a disguise. Nearby is a small hole in the rock through which a shifty-looking monkey-like ball of fur squeezes, thumbing its nose at the little cavern-house as it goes. The fur is the coat of a wolf and the shambler is an intelligent man-like being with short arms and bandy legs. It is shaped like an Orc but is fairer of face. Will you steal into the cavern-house (turn to **29**) or follow the shambler through the hole (turn to **49**)?

420

From the Worldworm's maw you plunge down a dark tunnel of ridged stone, towards its belly. But the Worldworm no longer has what pass for stomach and tail. Instead you fall out of a jagged hole in its body into a pitch-black void. The wind whistles past your ears as you fall ever faster into darkness.

The cries of the others sound below you. Cassandra tries to grab hold of you but loses her grip and you hear her cursing fervently in despair as her god will not help her. You try to call upon Kwon the Redeemer, and for a desperate moment you feel the presence of your god as he tries to lend you his strength, but it is only a moment. You are too far from the sunlit lands and still you fall.

Then you are wreathed in a gossamer thread, as smooth as silk, that slows your descent to the middle of Orb. You fall more slowly now, until at last you come gently to rest in a great cocoon of silk. A pale and sickly light looms above you and a great heaving body begins to scuttle closer to you on eight hairy black legs. You have fallen into the web of the Black Widow, whose minions have driven you to this pass. Here on the seventh tier you will make a juicy morsel for the Queen of Evil, unless you can master your despair and somehow rid Orb of its darkest blight...

*Avenger will return for new adventures in the seventh
Way of the Tiger book: **Redeemer!***

For more information:
www.megara-entertainment.com

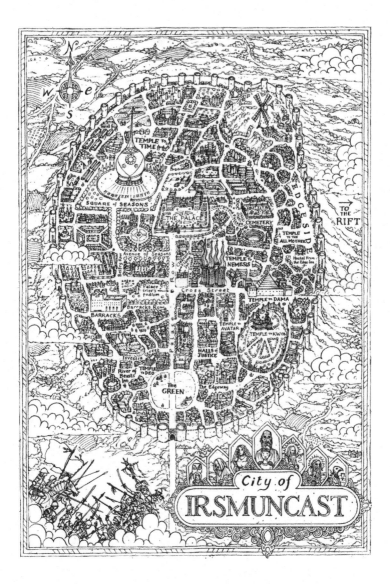

City of
IRSMUNCAST

If you enjoyed *Inferno* then you may like to try these other classic adventure gamebooks from Fabled Lands Publishing.

FABLED LANDS

A sweeping fantasy role-playing campaign in gamebook form

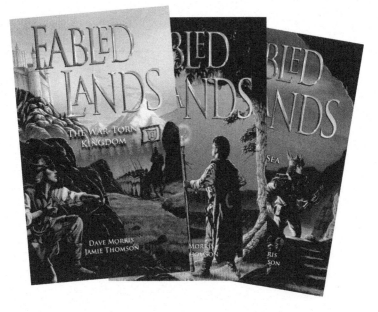

Set out on a journey of unlimited adventure!

FABLED LANDS is an epic interactive gamebook series with the scope of a massively multiplayer game world. You can choose to be an explorer, merchant, priest, scholar or soldier of fortune. You can buy a ship or a townhouse, join a temple, undertake desperate adventures in the wilderness or embroil yourself in court intrigues and the sudden violence of city backstreets. You can undertake missions that will earn you allies and enemies, or you can remain a free agent. With thousands of numbered sections to explore, the choices are all yours.